lonely planet

P9-CLI-306

BLUE RIDGE PARKWAY

ROAD TRIPS

Amy C Balfour, Virginia Maxwell,
Regis St Louis, Greg Ward

HOW TO USE THIS BOOK

Reviews

In the Destinations section:

All reviews are ordered in our authors' preference, starting with their most preferred option. Additionally:

Sights are arranged in the geographic order that we suggest you visit them and, within this order, by author preference.

Eating and Sleeping reviews are ordered by price range (budget, midrange, top end) and, within these ranges, by author preference.

Map Legend

Routes
Trip Route
Trip Detour
Linked Trip
Walk Route
Tollway
Freeway
Primary
Secondary
Tertiary
Lane
Unsealed Road
Plaza/Mall
Steps
)=(Tunnel
Pedestrian
  Overpass
Walk Track/Path

Boundaries
--- International
---- State/Province
----- Cliff

Hydrography
River/Creek
Intermittent River
Swamp/Mangrove
Canal
Water
Dry/Salt/
  Intermittent Lake
Glacier

Route Markers
[97] US National Hwy
[5] US Interstate Hwy
[44] State Hwy

Trips
[1] Trip Numbers
[9] Trip Stop
Walking tour
Trip Detour

Population
✪ Capital (National)
◉ Capital
  (State/Province)
● City/Large Town
○ Town/Village

Areas
Beach
Cemetery
  (Christian)
Cemetery (Other)
Park
Forest
Reservation
Urban Area
Sportsground

Transport
✈ Airport
Ⓑ BART station
Ⓣ Boston T station
Cable Car/
  Funicular
Ⓜ Metro/Muni station
Ⓟ Parking
Ⓢ Subway station
Train/Railway
Tram
Ⓤ Underground station

Note: Not all symbols displayed above appear on the maps in this book

Symbols In This Book

✓ Top Tips
🔗 Link Your Trips
💬 Tips from Locals
➦ Trip Detour
📖 History & Culture
👪 Family

🍷 Food & Drink
🌳 Outdoors
📷 Essential Photo
🏃 Walking Tour
✕ Eating
🛏 Sleeping

◉ **Sights**
🏖 **Beaches**
🏃 **Activities**
🎓 **Courses**
👉 **Tours**
✳ **Festivals & Events**

🛏 **Sleeping**
✕ **Eating**
🍷 **Drinking**
☆ **Entertainment**
🛍 **Shopping**
ⓘ **Information & Transportation**

These symbols and abbreviations give vital information for each listing:

☏ Telephone number
☺ Opening hours
Ⓟ Parking
⊖ Nonsmoking
❄ Air-conditioning
@ Internet access
📶 Wi-fi access
🏊 Swimming pool
🥗 Vegetarian selection
📖 English-language menu
👪 Family-friendly

🐾 Pet-friendly
🚌 Bus
⛴ Ferry
🚊 Tram
🚆 Train
apt apartments
 d double rooms
dm dorm beds
 q quad rooms
 r rooms
 s single rooms
ste suites
 tr triple rooms
 tw twin rooms

CONTENTS

PLAN YOUR TRIP

ROAD TRIPS

DESTINATIONS

ROAD TRIP ESSENTIALS.... 118

WELCOME TO
BLUE RIDGE PARKWAY

The Blue Ridge Parkway unfurls for 469 sumptuous miles, stretching from Virginia's Shenandoah National Park to North Carolina's Great Smoky Mountains. A national parkway, the lofty road rolls past a mountain landscape home to historic farms, scenic rivers, grazing wildlife, leafy trails and a lifetime's supply of waterfalls. Old-time mountain music can be heard regularly, and nearby wineries and craft breweries offer tastings on mountain slopes with sweeping views. What you won't find? Billboards or a single stoplight.

Vibrant mountain towns dot the foothills, bringing oomph to the party with delicious farm-to-table fare, one-of-a-kind arts and crafts, and story-filled inns.

With this book you'll buckle up for Parkway trips in Virginia and North Carolina, a cruise down Skyline Drive in Shenandoah National Park and a toe-tappin' trek along Virginia's Crooked Road Heritage Music Trail.

Blue Ridge Parkway in fall
ANTON ERMACHKOV / SHUTTERSTOCK ©

BLUE RIDGE PARKWAY

★

1 Skyline Drive
Classic American road trip studded with natural wonders and stunning scenery. **3 DAYS**

2 Blue Ridge Parkway: Virginia Verdant road that runs through the heart of the Appalachians. **3 DAYS**

4 Blue Ridge Parkway: North Carolina
This drive curves through the High Country, ending at the Smokies' doorstep. **5 DAYS**

3 Crooked Road
This music trail winds through the Blue Ridge Mountains into the Appalachians. **3–4 DAYS**

BLUE RIDGE PARKWAY

HIGHLIGHTS

★

Mountain Music (left) Lively fiddle-and-banjo tunes drift over hills and hollers at outdoor music venues across the Blue Ridge Mountains. Hear it on Trips **1** and **3**.

Mt Mitchell State Park (above) Catch some serious air at the highest point on the parkway and watch the best sunset east of the Mississippi. See it on Trip **4**.

Asheville (right) Hikers, bohemians, craft beer lovers and architecture buffs all converge in this vibrant mountain town. See it on Trip **4**.

CITY GUIDE

Roanoke skyline

ROANOKE

This former railroad town is finally embracing its outdoor bona fides. Flanked by the Blue Ridge Parkway, the Appalachian Trail and numerous lakes and waterways, Roanoke is working hard to promote itself as an ideal launchpad for regional adventures. Farm-to-table restaurants, new microbreweries and a burgeoning arts scene help make the case.

Getting Around

Valley Metro (www. valleymetro.com) runs the city bus service, which includes the free Star Line Trolley. The trolleys loop through downtown on weekdays (7am to 7pm) and connect shops, restaurants, lodgings and several hospitals. Pedestrian- and cyclist-friendly greenways (www. greenways.org) crisscross the city.

Parking

On-street parking downtown is typically easy to find and there are several large garages near the City Market Building (www.citymarketbuilding.

com). At metered spots the first hour is free, the second hour is $1. The cost for three hours, the maximum time allowed, is $4.

Where to Eat

There are numerous good eating and drinking options downtown. Many can be found in the City Market Building and along surrounding streets. Others are found in suburban shopping strips in Crystal Spring and Grandin Village.

Where to Stay

National chain hotels are located near the airport and there's a historic hotel

downtown. There's great camping in the nearby Blue Ridge Mountains, with several nice spots along the Appalachian Trail.

Useful Websites

Visit Roanoke (www. visitroanoakeva.com) City tourism website.

Roanoke Outside (www. roanokeoutside.com) Outdoor opportunities across the region.

Trips through Roanoke:

2 **3**

Destination Coverage: p75

Battery Park Ave, Asheville

ASHEVILLE

Hikers, cyclists and road trippers descend from the mountains to unwind in downtown Asheville. In this overgrown mountain town, innovative chefs create culinary masterpieces while small-batch breweries bring good cheer. Sidewalk buskers provide the background music. The Biltmore shares the good life – for a fee.

Getting Around

The 18 local bus routes run by Asheville Transit (ART) typically operate between 5:30am and 10:30pm Monday through Saturday, and shorter hours Sunday. Tickets cost $1, and there are free bike racks. Route S3 connects the downtown ART station with Asheville Regional Airport.

Parking

Although there's very little free parking downtown, public garages are free for the first hour and only cost $1 per hour thereafter. The handy Passport app (https://passportinc.com) facilitates paying for Asheville's parking meters and paid lots.

Where to Eat

Downtown and South Slope burst with enticing options, including simple (but trendy) Southern-fried cafes, diners and elaborate Modern American and Appalachian kitchens. Local, organic and sustainable are mantras. With more alternatives in the River Arts District and in West Asheville, you won't starve in these mountains.

Where to Stay

To be within walking distance of South Slope microbreweries, top restaurants, good music venues and the best shops, you'll need to stay downtown, where prices are high and choices limited. Cheaper chain motels line the interstates. For posher digs, head to the Grove Park Inn or lodgings on the Biltmore Estate.

Useful Websites

Explore Asheville (www. exploreasheville.com) Tourism website for the city.

Asheville Ale Trail (www. ashevillealetrail.com) Guide to the city's breweries.

Trips through Asheville:

4

Destination Coverage: p86

11

NEED TO KNOW

CELL PHONES
The only foreign phones that work in the USA are GSM multiband models. Cell phone reception can be spotty in the mountains.

FUEL
There are no gas stations along the Blue Ridge Parkway, but they are common in nearby towns. Gasoline is available on Skyline Drive at the Big Meadows Wayside (Mile 51). Small-town stations may be open only from 7am to 8pm or 9pm.

RENTAL CARS
Budget (www.budget.com)

Enterprise (www.enterprise.com)

National (www.nationalcar.com)

IMPORTANT NUMBERS
AAA (☎800-222-4357) Roadside Assistance

Blue Ridge Parkway Information (☎828-298-0398)

Directory Assistance (☎411)

Emergency (☎911)

Shenandoah National Park Information (☎540-999-3500)

Climate

Warm to hot summers, cold winters
Warm to hot summers, mild winters

Washington, DC
GO Mar–Apr, Sep–Oct

Roanoke, VA
GO May–Oct

Richmond, VA
GO Apr–Oct

Asheville, NC
GO Apr–Nov

Charlotte, NC
GO Mar–May, Sep–Nov

When to Go

High Season (Jun–Aug)
» Warm, sunny days across the region.

» Accommodation prices peak (up 30% on average).

» Outdoor bluegrass and mountain music shows are common.

Shoulder Season (Apr–May, Sep–Oct)
» Milder temperatures; can be rainy.

» Wildflowers bloom, especially in May.

» Fall foliage draws crowds.

Low Season (Nov–Mar)
» Dark, wintry days with moderate snowfall.

» Lowest prices for accommodations.

» Attractions keep shorter hours or close for winter.

Daily Costs

Budget: Less than $100
» Dorm bed: $30–55
» Campsite: $15–30
» Budget motel room: $60–80
» Lunch from cafe or food truck: $8–15
» Travel on public transport: $0–5

Midrange: $150–250
» Room in a midrange hotel: $80–200
» Dinner in a popular restaurant: $20–40
» Car rental per day: from $30

Top end: More than $250
» Room in a top hotel/resort: from $250
» Dinner in a top restaurant: $60–100
» Big night out (plays, concerts, clubs): $60–200

Eating

Diners Informal with cheap breakfasts and lunches.

Cafes Open typically during the daytime; good to relax over a good lunch in an engaging setting.

Brewpubs & Gastropubs Regional craft beers and wines with good pub grub.

Top-end restaurants Include some of the highest rated chef-driven restaurants in the region.

The following price ranges refer to a main course.

$ less than $15
$$ $15–$30
$$$ more than $30

Sleeping

B&Bs A good choice in small towns.

Cabins & Cottages Cabins are abundant.

Historic Inns Well done in small cities in the mountain foothills.

Hotels & Motels You'll find indie-owned gems in touristy regions and mountain towns.

The price ranges below are for a double room in high season, before taxes and tips.

$ less than $150
$$ $150–$250
$$$ more than $250

Arriving in Virginia & North Carolina

Washington Dulles International Airport
Bus Silver Line Express runs every 15 to 20 minutes from Dulles to Wiehle-Reston East Metro station between 6am and 10:40pm (from 7:45am weekends). Total time to the center of Washington, DC is 60 to 75 minutes, total cost around $11.

Taxi Costs $62 to $73.

Roanoke-Blacksburg Regional Airport
Car 5 miles north of downtown; I-81 and I-581 link to the city.

Asheville Regional Airport
Bus Route S3 runs to Asheville Transit Hub 10 times daily.

Car The airport is 16 miles south of Asheville.

Internet Access

Wi-fi is common in lodgings across the price spectrum. Many properties have an internet-connected computer for public use. Many restaurants and cafes offer free wi-fi.

Money

ATMs are available at the lodges on Skyline Drive. The only ATM on the parkway is at the Peaks of Otter Lodge (p29) in Virginia. ATMs are numerous in nearby towns. If you're camping without prior reservations, bring small bills for the self-pay kiosks.

Tipping

Tipping is expected and not optional. Tip 15% to 20% at restaurants, 10%-15% for bartenders and taxi drivers, and $2 per bag for porters.

Opening Hours

Weather permitting, the Blue Ridge Parkway and Shenandoah National Park are open 24/7 year-round.

Visitor Centers Most visitor centers on the Parkway are open daily from mid-May through September or October (typically 10am-5pm). The Byrd Visitor Center (p69) is open year-round.

Campgrounds The eight campgrounds along the Blue Ridge Parkway are open from May through late October. Campgrounds in Shenandoah National Park open in the spring and close in late fall.

For more, see Driving in the USA (p118).

Road Trips

1 Skyline Drive 3 Days
Skyline Drive is one of America's classic road trips. Befittingly, it comes studded like a leather belt with natural wonders and stunning scenery. (p17)

2 Blue Ridge Parkway: Virginia 3 Days
Dark laurel, fragrant galax, white waterfalls and many blooms line this road that runs through the heart of the Appalachians. (p25)

3 Crooked Road 3–4 Days
On this trip, you can discover the music and folkways of the forested upcountry between the Blue Ridge and Appalachian mountain ranges. (p33)

4 Blue Ridge Parkway: North Carolina 5 Days
This drive curves through the High Country, climbs the East Coast's highest peak, then ends at the Smokies' doorstep. (p43)

View of Grandfather Mountain and Pisgah National Forest from near Boone (p83)
CVANDYKE / SHUTTERSTOCK ©

Skyline Drive

Skyline Drive is one of America's classic road trips. Befittingly, it comes studded like a leather belt with natural wonders and stunning scenery.

1

TRIP HIGHLIGHTS

Dinosaur Land

Front Royal **START**

● Huntly

42 miles

Mathews Arm & Elkwallow
Tall waterfalls and peaceful picnic spots

61 miles

Luray
Deep caverns cut into the Earth

⑤

⑥

⑨

⑩

Lewis Mountain
FINISH

85 miles

Hawksbill Area
Strain your neck staring up at the tallest Shenandoah peak

Byrd Visitor Center
Dedicated to local culture and nature

95 miles

**3 DAYS
150 MILES/240KM**

GREAT FOR...

BEST TIME TO GO

From May to November for great weather, open facilities and clear views.

ESSENTIAL PHOTO

The fabulous 360-degree horizon at the top of Bearfence Mountain.

BEST FOR CULTURE

Byrd Visitor Center offers an illuminating peek into Appalachian folkways.

Left View from Hawksbill (p22)

17

1 Skyline Drive

The centerpiece of the ribbon-thin Shenandoah National Park is the jaw-dropping beauty of Skyline Drive, which runs for just over 100 miles atop the Blue Ridge Mountains. Unlike the massive acreage of western parks like Yellowstone or Yosemite, Shenandoah is at times only a mile wide. That may seem to narrow the park's scope, yet it makes it a perfect space for traversing and road-tripping goodness.

1 Front Royal

Straddling the northern entrance to the park is the tiny city of Front Royal. Although it's not among Virginia's fanciest ports of call, this lush riverside town offers all the urban amenities you might need before a camping or hiking trip up in the mountains.

If you need to gather your bearings, start at the **Front Royal Visitor Center** (📞800-338-2576, 540-635-5788; www.discov-erfrontroyal.com; 414 E Main St; ⏰9am-5pm). Friendly

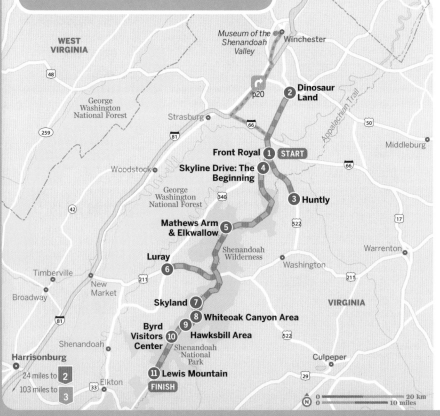

staff are on hand to overwhelm you with information about what to do in the area.

The Drive » Dinosaur Land is 10 miles north of Front Royal, towards Winchester, via US 340 (Stonewall Jackson Hwy).

❷ Dinosaur Land

Before you head into the national park and its stunning natural beauty, visit **Dinosaur Land** (☏540-869-2222; www.dinosaurland.com; 3848 Stonewall Jackson Hwy, White Post; adult/child 2-10yr $6/5; ⏱9:30am-5:30pm Mar-May, to 6pm Jun-Aug, to 5pm Sep & Oct; 👶) for some fantastic man-made tackiness. This spectacularly low-brow shrine to concrete sculpture is not to be missed. Although it's an 'educational prehistoric

LINK YOUR TRIP

2 **Blue Ridge Parkway: Virginia**

You can head from the park exit to Staunton, VA, about 20 minutes away, to start 'America's Favorite Drive.'

3 **Crooked Road** From the southern tip of Skyline Drive, follow I-81 south 100 miles to Roanoke for mountain music.

forest,' with more than 50 life-size dinosaurs (and a King Kong for good measure), you'd probably learn more about the tenants by fast-forwarding through *Jurassic Park 3*. But that's not why you've stopped here, so grab your camera and sidle up to the triceratops for memories that will last a millennium.

The Drive » Head back to Front Royal, then go south on US 522 (Remount Rd) for about 9 miles to reach Huntly.

❸ Huntly

Huntly is a small-ish town nestled in the green foothills of the Shenandoahs, lying just in the southern shadows of Front Royal. It's a good spot to refuel on some cosmopolitan culture and foodie deliciousness in the form of **Rappahannock Cellars** (☏540-635-9398; www.rappahannockcellars.com; 14437 Hume Rd; wine tasting $10, spirits tasting $13; ⏱11:30am-5pm Sun-Fri, to 6pm Sat), one of the nicer wineries of north-central Virginia, where vineyard-covered hills shadow the horizon, like some slice of northern Italian pastoral prettiness that got lost somewhere in the upcountry of the Old Dominion. Give the port a whirl (well, maybe not if you're driving).

The Drive » Head back to Front Royal, as you'll enter Skyline Drive from there. From

the beginning of Skyline Drive, it's 5.5 miles to Dickey Ridge.

❹ Skyline Drive: The Beginning

Skyline Drive is the scenic drive to end all scenic drives. The 75 overlooks, with views into the Shenandoah Valley and the Piedmont, are all breathtaking. In spring and summer, endless variations on the color green are sure to enchant, just as the vibrant reds and yellows will amaze you in autumn. This might be your chance to finally hike a section of the Appalachian Trail, which crosses Skyline Drive in 32 places.

The logical first stop on an exploration of Skyline Drive and Shenandoah National Park is the Dickey Ridge Visitor Center (p69). It's not just an informative leaping-off point; it's a building with a fascinating history all of its own. This spot originally operated as a 'wild' dining hall in 1908 (back then that simply meant it had a terrace for dancing). However, it closed during WWII and didn't reopen until 1958, when it became a visitor center. Now it's one of the park's two main information centers and contains a little bit of everything you'll need to get started on your trip along Skyline Drive.

The Drive » It's a twisty 19 more miles along Skyline Drive to Mathews Arm.

⑤ Mathews Arm & Elkwallow

Mathews Arm is the first major section of Shenandoah National Park you encounter after leaving Dickey Ridge. Before you get there, you can stop at a pullover at Mile 19.4 and embark on a 4.8-mile loop hike to **Little Devils Stairs.** Getting through this narrow gorge is as tough as the name suggests; expect hand-over-hand climbing for some portions.

At Mathews Arm there's a campground as well as an amphitheater, and some nice breezes; early on in your drive, you're already at a 2750ft altitude.

From the amphitheater, it's a 6.5-mile round-trip, moderately taxing hike to lovely **Overall Run Falls**, the tallest in the national park (93ft). There are plenty of rock ledges where you can enjoy the view and snap a picture, but be warned that the falls sometimes dry out in the summer.

Elkwallow Wayside, which includes a nice picnic area and lookout, is at Mile 24, just past Mathews Arm.

The Drive » From Mathews Arm, proceed south along Skyline for about 10 miles, then take the US 211 ramp westbound for about 7 miles to reach Luray.

⑥ Luray

Luray is a good spot to grab some grub and potentially rest your head if you're not into camping. It's also where you'll find the wonderful **Luray Caverns** (☎540-743-6551; www.luraycaverns.com; 970 US Hwy 211 W; adult/child 6-12yr $27/14; ☉9am-7pm daily mid-Jun–Aug, to 6pm Sep-Nov & Apr–mid-Jun, to 4pm Mon-Fri, to 5pm Sat & Sun Dec-Mar), one of the most extensive cavern systems on the East Coast.

Here you can take a one-hour, roughly 1-mile guided tour of the caves, opened to the public more than 100 years ago. The rock formations throughout are quite stunning, and Luray boasts what is surely a one-of-a-kind attraction – the Stalacpipe Organ – in the pit of its belly. This crazy contraption has been banging out melodies on the rock formations for decades. As the guide says, the caves are 400 million years old '*if* you believe in geological dating' (this is a conservative part of the country where Creationism is widely accepted, if hotly debated). No matter what you believe in, you'll be impressed by the fantastic underground expanses.

DETOUR: MUSEUM OF THE SHENANDOAH VALLEY

Start: ① Front Royal

Of all the places where you can begin your journey into Shenandoah National Park, none seem to make quite as much sense as the **Museum of the Shenandoah Valley** (☎888-556-5799, 540-662-1473; www.themsv.org; 901 Amherst St, Winchester; adult/student 13-18yr/child $10/8/free, Wed free; ☉10am-5pm Tue-Sun Apr-Dec, 11am-4pm Jan-Mar), an institution dedicated to its namesake. Located in the town of Winchester, some 25 miles north of Front Royal, the museum is an exhaustive repository of information on the valley, Appalachian culture and its associated folkways, some of the most unique in the USA. Exhibits are divided into four galleries, accompanied by the restored Glen Burnie historical home and six acres of gardens.

To get here, take I-66 west from Front Royal to I-81 and head north for 25 miles. In Winchester, follow signs to the museum, which is on the outskirts of town.

Stalacpipe Organ in Luray Caverns

The Drive » Take US 211 east for 10 miles to get back on Skyline Drive. Then proceed 10 miles south along Skyline to get to Skyland. Along the way you'll drive over the highest point of Skyline Drive (3680ft). At Mile 40.5, just before reaching Skyland, you can enjoy amazing views from the parking overlook at Thorofare Mountain (3595ft).

7 Skyland (p66)

Horse-fanciers will want to book a trail ride through Shenandoah at **Skyland Stables** (☎855-470-6005; www.goshenandoah. com; Mile 42.5, Skyline Dr; guided group rides 1-/2½-hr $50/95; ☻9am-5pm Apr-Oct). Rides last up to two-and-

a-half hours and are a great way to see the wild-life and epic vistas. Pony rides are also available for the wee members of your party. This is a good spot to break up your trip if you're into hiking (and if you're on this trip, we're assuming you are).

You've got great access to local trail heads around here, and the sunsets are fabulous. The accommodations are a little rustic, but in a charming way (the Trout Cabin was built in 1911 and it feels like it, but we mean this in the most complimentary way possible.) The place positively oozes nos-

talgia, but if you're into amenities, you may find it a little dilapidated.

The Drive » It's only 1.5 miles south on Skyline Drive to get to the Whiteoak parking area.

8 Whiteoak Canyon Area

At Mile 42.6, Whiteoak Canyon is another area of Skyline Drive that offers unmatched hiking and exploration opportunities. There are several parking areas that all provide different entry points to the various trails that snake through this ridge- and stream-scape.

Most hikers are attracted to Whiteoak Canyon for its **waterfalls** – there are six in total, with the tallest topping out at 86ft. At the Whiteoak parking area, you can make a 4.6-mile round trip hike to these cascades, but know that it's a both a steep climb up and back to your car. To reach the next set of waterfalls, you'll have to add 2.7 miles to the round trip and prepare yourself for a steep (1100ft) elevation shift.

The **Limberlost Trail** and parking area is just south of Whiteoak Canyon. This is an easy 1.3-mile circuit trek into spruce upcountry thick with hawks, owls and other birds. The boggy ground is home to many salamanders. The trail is wheelchair accessible.

The Drive ›› It's about 3 miles south of Whiteoak Canyon to the Hawksbill area via Skyline Drive.

TRIP HIGHLIGHT

9 Hawksbill Area (p66)

Once you reach Mile 45.6, you've reached **Hawksbill**, the name of both this part of Skyline Drive and the tallest peak in Shenandoah National Park. Numerous trails in this area skirt the summits of the mountain.

Pull into the parking area at Hawksbill Gap (Mile 45.6). You've got a few hiking options to pick from. The **Lower Hawksbill Trail** is a steep 1.7-mile round trip that circles Hawksbill's lower slopes. The huff-inducing ascent yields a pretty great view over the park. Another great lookout lays at the end of the **Upper Hawksbill Trail**, a moderately difficult 2.1-mile trip. You can link up with the Appalachian Trail here via a spur called the Salamander Trail.

If you continue south for about 5 miles you'll reach **Fishers Gap Overlook**. The attraction here is the **Rose River Loop**, a 4-mile, moderately strenuous trail that is positively Edenic. Along the way you'll pass by waterfalls, under thick forest canopy and over swift-running streams.

DANIEL REINER / SHUTTERSTOCK ©

The Drive ›› From Fishers Gap, head about a mile south to the Byrd Visitor Center, technically located at Mile 51.

TRIP HIGHLIGHT

10 Byrd Visitor Center

The Harry F Byrd Visitor Center (p69) is the central visitor center of Shenandoah National Park, marking (roughly) a halfway point between the two ends of Skyline Drive. It's devoted to explaining the settlement and development of Shenandoah Valley via a series of small but well-curated exhibitions; as such, it's

GARDEN MAZE ALERT

Next to the Luray Caverns is an excellent opportunity to let your inner Shelley Duvall or Scatman Crothers run wild. Go screaming *Shining*-style through the **Garden Maze**, but beware! This maze is harder than it looks and some could spend longer inside it than they anticipated. Paranormal and psychic abilities are permitted, but frowned upon, when solving the hedge maze. Redrum! Redrum!

Horseback riding around Skyline Drive

a good place to stop and learn about the surrounding culture (and pick up backcountry camping permits). There are camping and ranger activities in the **Big Meadows** area, located across the road from the visitor center.

The **Story of the Forest** trail is an easy, paved, 1.8-mile loop that's quite pretty; the trailhead connects to the visitor center. You can also explore two nearby waterfalls. **Dark Hollow Falls**, which sounds (and looks) like something out of a Tolkien novel, is a 70ft high cascade located at the end of a quite steep 1.4-mile trail. **Lewis Falls**, accessed via Big Meadows, is on a moderately difficult 3.3-mile trail that intersects the Appalachian Trail; at one point you'll be scrabbling up a rocky slope.

The Drive ›› The Lewis Mountain area is about 5 miles south of the Byrd Visitor Center via Skyline Drive. Stop for good overlooks at Milam Gap and Naked Creek (both clearly signposted from the road).

⑪ Lewis Mountain

Lewis Mountain is both the name of one of the major camping areas of Shenandoah National Park and a nearby 3570ft mountain. The trail to the mountain is only about a mile long (round trip) with a small elevation gain, and leads to a nice overlook. But the best view here is from the top of **Bearfence Mountain**. This 1.2-mile circuit hike gets steep and rocky, and you don't want to attempt it during or after rainfall. The reward is one of the best panoramas of the Shenandoahs. After you leave, remember there's still about 50 miles of Skyline Drive between you and the park exit at Rockfish Gap.

Blue Ridge Parkway: Virginia

Dark laurel, fragrant galax, white waterfalls and blooms of dogwood, mayapple, foamflower and redbud line this road that runs through the heart of the Appalachians.

2

TRIP HIGHLIGHTS

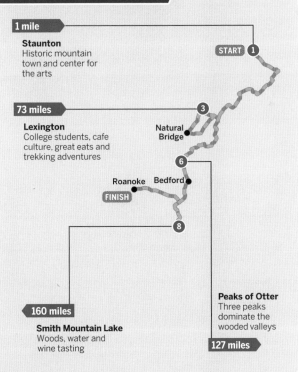

1 mile

Staunton
Historic mountain town and center for the arts

START 1

73 miles

Lexington
College students, cafe culture, great eats and trekking adventures

3

Natural Bridge

6

Roanoke Bedford

FINISH

8

160 miles

Smith Mountain Lake
Woods, water and wine tasting

Peaks of Otter
Three peaks dominate the wooded valleys

127 miles

**3 DAYS
216 MILES/347KM**

GREAT FOR...

BEST TIME TO GO

Visit June through October for great weather and open amenities.

ESSENTIAL PHOTO

A panorama of the Blue Ridge Mountains from Sharp Top, Peaks of Otter.

BEST FOR CULTURE

Staunton is a food and arts hub.

Left Natural Bridge (p28)

25

2

Blue Ridge Parkway: Virginia

Rolling through Virginia and North Carolina, the Blue Ridge National Scenic Byway – 'America's Favorite Drive' – is the most visited area of national parkland in the USA, attracting almost 20 million road-trippers a year. On this trip we'll thread on and off the parkway in Virginia, passing bucolic pasturelands, imposing Appalachian vistas, charming college towns and several great hiking trails.

TRIP HIGHLIGHT

1 Staunton (p69)

This trip starts in a place we'd like to end. End up retiring, that is. There are some towns in the USA that just, for lack of a better term, *nail it*, and Staunton is one of them. Luckily, it serves as a good base for exploring the upper parkway.

What's here? A pedestrian-friendly and handsome center; more than 200 of the town's buildings were designed by noted Victorian archi-

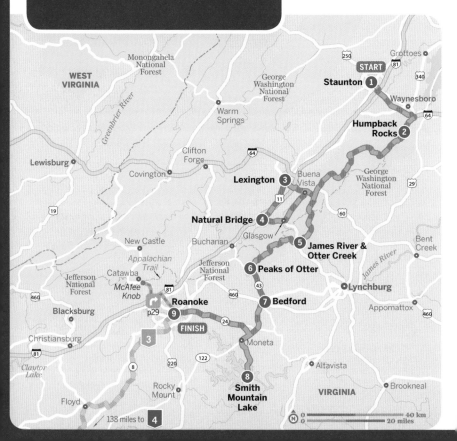

tect TJ Collins, hence Staunton's attractive uniformity. There's an artsy yet unpretentious bohemian vibe thanks to the presence of two things: Mary Baldwin – a small women's liberal arts college – and the gem of the Shenandoah Mountains: Blackfriars Playhouse (p71). This is the world's only re-creation of Shakespeare's original indoor theater. The facility hosts the immensely talented American Shakespeare Center company, with performances throughout the year. See a show here. It will do you good.

History buffs should check out the **Woodrow Wilson Presidential Library** (☎540-885-0897; www.woodrowwilson.org; 18 N Coalter St; adult/student/child 6-12yr $14/7/5; ⏰9am-5pm Mon-Sat, from noon Sun Mar-Oct, to 4pm Nov-Feb) across

LINK YOUR TRIP

 Crooked Road
In Roanoke, slip on dancing clogs and explore regional folkways and backroads.

 Blue Ridge Parkway: North Carolina
Tunnels abound on the parkway and a mile-high swinging bridge awaits on Grandfather Mountain.

town. Stop by and tour the hilltop Greek Revival house where Wilson grew up, which has been faithfully restored to its original 1856 appearance.

The hard work of farming comes to life at the Frontier Culture Museum (p69) via the familiar Virginia trope of employing historically costumed interpreters. The museum has Irish, German and English farm houses to explore.

The Drive ≫ From Staunton, take I-64E towards Richmond for about 15 miles. Take exit 99 to merge onto US 250/Three Notched Mountain Hwy heading east toward Afton, then follow the signs onto the Blue Ridge Parkway. Humpback Rocks is at Mile 5.8.

---

② Humpback Rocks

Had enough great culture and small-town hospitality? No? Tough, because we're moving on to the main event: the Blue Ridge Parkway. To be honest, this is a weird trip. We're asking you to drive along the parkway, which slowly snakes across the peaks of the Appalachians, but every now and then we're going to ask you to detour off this scenic mountain road to, well, other scenic roads.

Anyways, we start at **Humpback Rocks** (www.nps.gov/blri; Mile 5.8, Blue Ridge Pkwy), the entrance to the Virginia portion of the parkway (252 miles of the 469-mile parkway are

in North Carolina). You can tour 19th-century farm buildings or take the steep trail to the namesake Humpback Rocks, which offer spectacular 360-degree views across the mountains. The round-trip hike is 2 miles. The onsite **visitor center** is a good primer for the rest of your parkway experience. Old-time bands play mountain music on the lawn by the visitor center every Sunday afternoon from late May through September.

The Drive ≫ The next stretch of the trip is 39 miles on the parkway. Follow signs for US 60, then follow that road west for 10 miles to Lexington.

TRIP HIGHLIGHT

③ Lexington (p71)

What? Another attractive university town set amid the forested mountains of the lower Shenandoah Valley? Well, why not.

In fact, while Staunton moderately revolves around Mary Baldwin, Lexington positively centers, geographically and culturally, around two schools: the Virginia Military Institute (VMI; p72) and Washington & Lee University (W&L; p72). VMI is the oldest state-supported military academy in the country, dedicated to producing the Classical ideal of citizen-soldiers; the ideals of this institution and the history of its cadet-students are explored at the VMI Museum (p72). While graduates do not have to become enlisted officers within the US military, the vast majority do so. In addition, the school's George C Marshall Museum (p72) honors the creator of the Marshall Plan for post-WWII European reconstruction.

VMI cadets can often be seen jogging around Lexington, perhaps casting a glance at the students at Washington & Lee, a decidedly less structured but no less academically respected school. The W&L campus includes the Lee Chapel & Museum (p72), where the school's namesake, patron and Confederate general Robert E Lee is buried. Lee's beloved horse, Traveller, is buried outside, and visitors often leave pennies as a sign of respect.

Just a few miles north on Rte 11 is Hull's Drive-in movie theater (p74). This totally hardcore artifact of the golden age of automobiles is a living museum to the road trips your parents remember.

The Drive » Take US 11 southbound for about 12 miles to get to Natural Bridge (you can take I-81 as well, but it's not nearly as scenic and takes just as long).

----

4 Natural Bridge

Before we send you back to the Blue Ridge Parkway, stop by the gorgeous **Natural Bridge** (☏540-291-1326; www.dcr.virginia.gov; 6477 S Lee Hwy; adult/child 6-12yr $8/6; ◷9am-5pm). The limestone arch, praised by Thomas Jefferson himself, is a legitimate natural wonder – and is even claimed to be one of the Seven Natural Wonders of the World, though just who put that list together remains unclear. Soaring 215ft in the air, this centuries-old rock formation lives up to the hype. Those who aren't afraid of a little religion can check out the independently run **'Drama of Creation' light show** (www.naturalbridgeva.com/attractions; $3 per person) that plays most nights underneath and around the bridge. Natural Bridge, formerly privately owned, became a state park in 2016.

The Drive » Head back to the Blue Ridge Parkway using US 60 and get on at Buena Vista. Drive about 13 miles south to the James River area near Mile 63.

----

5 James River & Otter Creek

The next portion of the Blue Ridge Parkway overlooks the road leading to Lynchburg. Part of the reason for that town's proximity is the James River, which marks the parkway's lowest elevation (650ft above sea level). The river was the original transportation route through the mountains.

This area is rife with hiking and sightseeing opportunities. **Otter Creek Trail** begins at a local campsite and runs for a moderately strenuous 3.5 miles; you can access it at different points from overlooks at Mile 61.4, Mile 62.5 and Mile 63.1.

For an easy jaunt, head to the **James River Visitor Center** at Mile 63.6 and take the 0.2-mile

---

CAMPGROUNDS

There are numerous private camping sites near the parkway. Four public **campgrounds** (☏877-444-6777; www.recreation.gov; Mile 89.5, Blue Ridge Pkwy; tent & RV sites $20; ◷May-late Oct), located at Mile 60.8, Mile 85.6, Mile 120.4 and Mile 161.1, can be found on the Virginia side of the Blue Ridge Parkway. These parkway campgrounds are open from May to October; book online. Demand is higher on weekends and holidays. While there are no electrical hookups at parkway campsites, you will find restrooms, potable water and picnic tables. You're often at a pretty high elevation (over 2500ft), so even during summer it can get chilly up here.

James River Trail to the restored James River and Kanawha Canal lock, built between 1845 and 1851. The visitor center has information on the history of the canal and its importance to local transportation. From here follow the **Trail of Trees**, which goes half a mile to a wonderful overlook on the James River.

The Drive » It's about 20 miles from here to Peaks of Otter along the parkway. At Mile 74.7, the very easy, 0.1-mile Thunder Ridge Trail leads to a pretty valley view. Access the tough 1.2-mile Apple Orchard Falls Trail at Mile 78.4.

- - - - - - - - - - - - - - - -

`TRIP HIGHLIGHT`

6 Peaks of Otter

The three **Peaks of Otter** – Sharp Top, Flat Top and Harkening Hill – were once declared the highest mountains in North America by Thomas Jefferson. His assessment was wrong, but the peaks are undeniably dramatic, dominating the landscape for miles around.

From the visitor center at Mile 86 you can take the steep 1.5-mile **Sharp Top Trail** (one-way), which summits the eponymous mountain (3875ft) and offers impressive 360-degree views of the mountain-and-piedmont landscape. The **Flat Top Trail** goes higher and further (5.4 miles roundtrip), but at a less demanding incline. The 0.8-mile **Elk Run Trail** is an easy self-

Peaks of Otter Lodge

guided loop and nature tour. For the history of an early 1900s' apple farm, check out the **Johnson Farm** off the short Johnson Farm Trail.

At Mile 83.1, before the visitor center, the **Fallingwater Cascades Trail** is a 1.5-mile loop that wanders past deep-carved ravines to a snowy-white waterfall.

The **Peaks of Otter Lodge** sits prettily beside a lake at the base of the peaks. The gift shop sells an amusing bumper sticker that says 'POO' – the abbreviation for Peaks of Otter.

The Drive » Get on VA-43 south, also known as Peaks Rd, from the Blue Ridge Parkway. It's about an 11-mile drive to Bedford.

↱ DETOUR: MCAFEE KNOB

Start: 9 Roanoke

This dramatic rock ledge is one of the most photographed sights on the Appalachian Trail, offering a sweeping view of Catawba Valley and surrounding mountains. The ledge is a 4.4-mile climb from the trailhead, which is 16 miles northwest of downtown Roanoke. To get there, take I-581 N to I-81 S, following the latter to Exit 141. From there, take Hwy 419 N to Rte 311. It's 5.5 miles to the trailhead parking lot atop Catawba Mountain.

⑦ Bedford

Tiny Bedford suffered the most casualties per capita during WWII, and hence was chosen to host the **National D-Day Memorial** (☎540-586-3329; www.dday.org; 3 Overlord Circle; adult/student 6yr-college $10/6; ☺10am-5pm, closed Mon Dec-Feb). Among its towering arch and flower garden is a cast of bronze figures re-enacting the storming of the beach, complete with bursts of water symbolizing the hail of bullets the soldiers faced.

The surrounding countryside is speckled with vineyards. **Peaks of Otter Winery** (☎540-586-3707; www.peaksofotterwinery. com; 1218 Elmos Rd, Bedford; ☺noon-5pm daily Apr-Dec, Sat & Sun Jan-Mar) stands out from other viticulture tourism spots with its focus on producing fruit wines (the chili pepper wine is 'better for basting than tasting' according to management).

White Rock vineyards (☎540-890-3359; www.white rockwines.com; 2117 Bruno Dr, Goodview; ☺noon-5pm Thu-Mon Apr–mid-Dec) is a more traditional winery. A few acres of green grapevines (well, green in the right season anyway) seem to erupt around a pretty house. If you stop for a tasting, we're fans of the White Mojo pinot gris.

Learn more about the many vineyards here via the **Bedford Wine Trail** (www.thebedfordwine trail.com).

The Drive » Take VA-122 (Burks Hill Rd) southbound for about 13.5 miles. In Moneta, take a left onto State Route 608 and drive for 6 miles, then turn right onto Smith Mountain Lake Pkwy. Go 2 miles and you're at Smith Mountain Lake State Park.

TRIP HIGHLIGHT

⑧ Smith Mountain Lake

This enormous, 32-sq-mile reservoir is one of the most popular recreation spots in southwestern Virginia and the largest lake contained entirely within the borders of the commonwealth. Vacation rentals and water activities abound, as does development, and there are portions of this picturesque dollop that have been overwhelmed with rental units. Most

LOCAL KNOWLEDGE: DINOSAUR KINGDOM II

Ever heard of the mad professor Mark Cline? He used to create monsters for haunted house attractions in Virginia Beach. Then the spirit seized him and he moved a menagerie of weirdness – an army of 1950s-era movie matinee monster models – to the woods around Natural Bridge (p28) and displayed them at various venues along Route 11. The most well known of the bunch was Foamhenge, a life-sized replica of England's most famous mystery site built entirely out of Styrofoam,

Sadly, Foamhenge has moved to northern Virginia, and a major fire closed the other attractions. But don't despair! The wackiness recently returned with the opening of **Dinosaur Kingdom II** (☎540-464-2253; www.dinosaurkingdomii.com; 5781 S Lee Hwy, Lexington; adult/child 3-12yr $10/3; ☺11am-5pm Sat & Sun May & Sep-early Nov, 10am-6pm Jun-Aug; 🚸). Here, a revolving time tunnel transports visitors to a forest filled with Union soldiers trying – and failing – to use dinosaurs to defeat the Confederate army during the Civil War. The creations in this far-out kingdom are fun, wacky and eye-catching. We guarantee you'll smile. And dino-loving kids will dig it. Bring your camera.

BLUE RIDGE PARKWAY TRIP PLANNER

» There is no admission fee to drive the parkway or explore its trails.

» Driving the parkway is not so much a way to get from A to B as an experience to relish– don't expect to get anywhere fast.

» Distances are delineated by mileposts (MPs). The countdown starts around Mile 1 in Virginia, near Waynesboro, and continues all the way to Mile 469 near Cherokee, North Carolina.

» The speed limit is 45mph.

» Long stretches of the parkway close in winter, and may not reopen until March, while many visitor centers and campgrounds remain closed until May. Check the park-service website (www.nps.gov/blri) for more information.

» The North Carolina section of the parkway starts at Mile 216.9, between the Blue Ridge Mountain Center in Virginia and Cumberland Knob in North Carolina.

» There are 26 tunnels on the parkway in North Carolina, as opposed to just one in Virginia. Watch for signs to turn on your headlights.

» You can take your RV on the parkway. The lowest tunnel clearance is 10'6" near the parkway's terminus in Cherokee, NC.

» For more help with trip planning, check the websites of the Blue Ridge Parkway Association (www.blueridgeparkway.org) and the Blue Ridge National Heritage Area (www.blueridgeheritage.com).

lake access is via private property only.

This isn't the case at **Smith Mountain Lake State Park** (☏540-297-6066; www.dcr.virginia.gov/state-parks/smith-mountain-lake; 1235 State Park Rd, Huddleston; per vehicle $7; ⏱8:15am-dusk), located on the north shore of the lake. Don't get us wrong – there are lots of facilities here if you need them, including a boat ramp, picnic tables, fishing piers, an amphitheater, camping sites and cabin rentals. But in general, the area within the state park preserves the natural beauty of this

area. Thirteen hiking trails wind through the surrounding forests.

The nearby **Hickory Hill Winery** (☏540-296-1393; www.smlwine.com; 1722 Hickory Cove Lane, Moneta; ⏱noon-6pm Wed-Sun Apr-Oct, noon-5pm Sat Nov-Mar), anchored by a charming 1923 farmhouse, is a lovely spot to lounge about sipping on merlot either before or after your adventures on the lake.

The Drive » Head back toward Bedford on VA-122 and take a left on State Route 801/Stony Fork Rd. Follow this to VA-24/Stewartsville Rd and take that road west about 20 miles to Roanoke.

❾ Roanoke (p75)

Roanoke is the largest city and commercial hub of Southwest Virginia. It's not as picturesque as other towns, but it's a good logistical base. The busy Center in the Square (p75) is the city's cultural heartbeat, with a science museum and planetarium, local history museum and theater. The striking Taubman Museum of Art (p75), a few blocks away, hosts excellent temporary exhibits.

Roanoke is the start of Trip 3.

Crooked Road

On this trip, amateur anthropologists can discover the music and folkways of the forested upcountry between the Blue Ridge and Appalachian mountain ranges.

3

TRIP HIGHLIGHTS

200 miles

Abingdon
Preserved historic buildings and quirky bohemian population

45 miles

Floyd
Old-time music fans share the road with organic cuisine

START
Roanoke

Carter
Family Fold **9**

Bristol
FINISH

8

 3

Galax
The heart of southwest Virginia's bluegrass culture

108 miles

**3–4 DAYS
260 MILES/418KM**

GREAT FOR...

BEST TIME TO GO
Visit from May to October for great weather and a packed concert schedule.

ESSENTIAL PHOTO
The Friday-night bluegrass-palooza in 'downtown' Floyd.

 BEST FOR NATURE LOVERS
Hiking the forested loop of the Smart View trail.

3 Crooked Road

The place where Kentucky, Tennessee and Virginia kiss is a veritable hotbed of American roots music history, thanks to the vibrant cultural folkways of the Scots-Irish who settled the area in the 18th century. The Crooked Road – a state-created heritage music trail – carves a winding path through the Blue Ridge Mountains into the Appalachians and the heart of this way of life.

❶ Roanoke (p75)

This trip begins in Roanoke, the main urban hub of southwest Virginia, and continues along the Blue Ridge Parkway, explored in other trips. Roanoke is steadily becoming a regional cultural center, perhaps best exemplified by the presence of the Taubman Museum of Art (p75). The museum is set in a futuristic glass-and-steel structure inspired by the valley's natural beauty. Inside you'll find a wonderful collection of

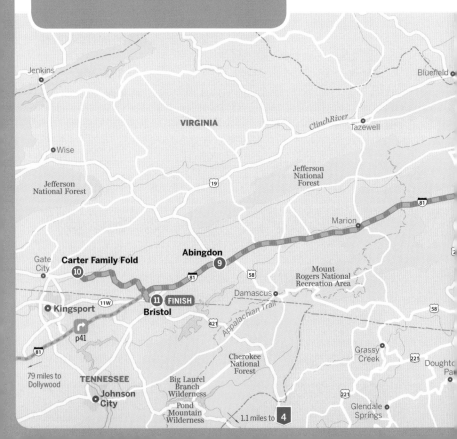

classic and modern art. The permanent collection includes extensive galleries of American, folk and contemporary Southern art, complemented by frequently rotating guest exhibitions whose thematic content spans the globe.

Before you leave, make sure to check out one of the finest farmer's markets in the region. The **Historic City Market** (☎540-342-2028; www.down townroanoke.org/city-market; Campbell Ave & Market St; ⏰8am-5pm; P) is a sumptuous affair spread out over several city blocks, loaded with temptations even for those with no access to a kitchen.

The Drive » Get onto US 220 southbound in Roanoke and follow signs to the Blue Ridge Parkway. It's about 33.5 miles from where US 220 hits the parkway to get to the Smart View Recreational Area.

❷ Smart View Recreational Area

The aptly named Smart View Recreational Area sits at an elevation of 2500ft with commanding vistas of the surrounding valleys. The area is a birder's parade, rife with trails that cut into

LINK YOUR TRIP

2 **Blue Ridge Parkway: Virginia**
From Roanoke, it's a short drive north to the striking Peaks of Otter. You will see deer along the way.

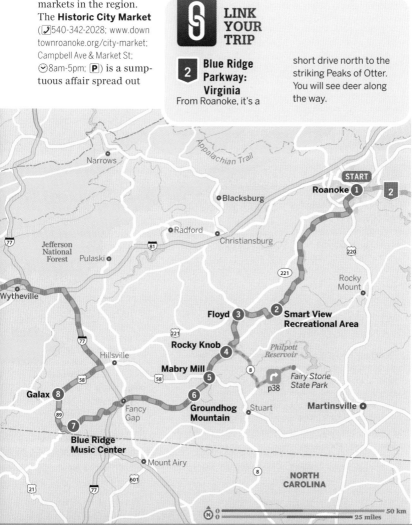

hardwood, broadleaf forest that teem with brown thrashers, great-crested flycatchers and Kentucky warblers, among many, many other species.

The **Smart View Trail** is a moderately difficult 2.6-mile loop that shows off the best of this area. If you're not in the mood (or don't have the time) to complete the entire circuit, the paths near the main parking pull-off for this area offer similar landscapes.

The Drive ≫ Continue along the Blue Ridge Parkway for 4 miles, then turn right onto State Route 860/Shooting Creek Rd. After about a mile, turn left onto State Route 681/Franklin Pike. Follow it for 2 miles, then turn left on Floyd Hwy.

TRIP HIGHLIGHT

③ Floyd (p77)

Tiny Floyd is a surprising blend of rural conservatives and slightly New Age artisans. Grab a double espresso from a bohemian coffeehouse,

then peruse farm tools in the hardware store.

The highlight of this curious town is the jamboree at the Floyd Country Store (p78). Every Friday night, this little store in a clapboard building clears out its inventory and lines up rows of chairs around a dance floor. Around 6:30pm the first musicians on the bill play their hearts out on the stage. Pretty soon the room's filled with locals and visitors dancing along with the fiddles and banjos.

Then the music spills out onto the streets. Several jam bands twiddle their fiddles in little groups up and down the main road. Listeners cluster round their favorite bands, parking themselves in lawn chairs right on the sidewalk or along the curb. Motorists stare at the scene in bewilderment. There's really nothing else like it. Just remember: this tradition

has been maintained as a family-friendly affair. Drinking, smoking and swearing are frowned upon.

The Drive ≫ Take VA-8/Locust St southbound for 6 miles back to the Blue Ridge Parkway. Then it's a little over 1.5 miles to Rocky Knob. If you follow VA-8, you can detour to Fairy Stone State Park.

④ Rocky Knob

At Rocky Knob, almost 1000ft higher than Smart View, rangers have carved out a 4800-acre area that blends natural beauty with landscaped amenities, including picnic areas and comfortable cabins.

If you're really looking to punish yourself and simultaneously soak up the best the Blue Ridge mountains have to offer, set out on the **Rock Castle Gorge Trail**, a hard-going, 10.8-mile loop that descends deep into the shadowed buttresses of Rock Castle Gorge before clambering out of the dark woods back into the sunlit slopes of Rocky Knob.

A much easier option is covering a small portion of the above via the 0.8-mile **Hardwood Cove Nature Trail**, which follows the beginning of the Rock Castle Gorge Trail and cuts under the dense canopies of some of the oldest forests in the Appalachians.

WILDFLOWER BLOOMS & FALL FOLIAGE

For information about spring blooms and fall colors along the parkway, call its seasonal hotline for the latest updates at ☏828-298-0398, ext 3. You'll also find a bloom calendar on the parkway website. Remember that flowers bloom and leaves change colors at different times based on elevation. Virginia is usually ahead of North Carolina when it comes to wildflower viewing due to the lower mountain elevations. Leaves begin to change color first at higher elevations, typically starting in early October.

Friday night at Floyd Country Store

DETOUR: FAIRY STONE STATE PARK

Start: 4 Rocky Knob

From the Rocky Knob portion of the Blue Ridge Parkway, head east for about 30 miles. You'll be passing through the upcountry region of Virginia that blends between the Blue Ridge mountains and the Southside, one of the most rural, least developed parts of the commonwealth. Marking the border between these regions is **Fairy Stone State Park** (☏276-930-2424; www.dcr.virginia.gov/state_parks/fai.shtml; 967 Fairystone Lake Dr, Stuart; per vehicle $5; ☺8am-10pm).

What's in a name? Well, the park grounds contain a silly amount of staurolite, a mineral that crystallizes at 60 or 90 degree angles, giving it a cross-like structure. Legend has it the cruciform rocks are the tears shed by fairies who learned of the death of Christ.

What else is here? Most folks come for 2880-acre **Philpott Lake**, created as a byproduct reservoir after the Army Corps of Engineers completed the Philpott Dam back in 1952. The mountain waters of the lake are a popular spot for swimming and fishing for smallmouth and largemouth bass. Some 10 miles of multi-use trails wend their way around the dark blue waters. There's also camping and cabins if you want to spend the night.

Get here by taking SR-758 south to US 58 eastbound; follow for 11 miles to VA-8. Take VA-8 to VA-57 and follow that road eastbound to Fairy Stone State Park.

The Drive » Mabry Mill is only a little over 3 miles south of Rocky Knob via the Blue Ridge Parkway, at Mile 176.

5 Mabry Mill

Here's where things go from picturesque Blue Ridge bucolic-ness to 'Oh, c'mon. Too cute.' Built in 1910, **Mabry Mill** (www.nps. gov/blri/planyourvisit/mabry-mill-mp-176.htm; 266 Mabry Mill Rd SE, Mile 176 off Blue Ridge Pkwy; ☺late May-late Oct) is a working water-wheel-driven grist mill. Its wooden construction has distressed over the years to a state of wonderful entropy; the structure looks like it just fell out of a historical ro-

mance novel, except you won't find a strapping young couple in a state of dramatic embrace in front of this building. The mill is managed by **Mabry Mill Restaurant** (☏276-952-2947; www. mabrymillrestaurant.com; breakfast mains $6-10, lunch & dinner mains $8-10; ☺7:30am-5pm Mon-Fri, to 6pm Sat & Sun late Apr-early Nov), which happens to whip up some of the better breakfasts along the Blue Ridge Parkway. It has three kinds of specialty pancakes - cornmeal, buckwheat and sweet potato. Throw in a biscuit with some Virginia ham and it's a perfect way to start your day.

Three miles down the road, at Mile 179, the half-mile **Round Meadow Creek Loop Trail** leads trekkers through a lovely forest cut through by an achingly attractive stream.

The Drive » Continue on from Mabry Mill to the Groundhog Mountain Picnic Area, which is 0.8 miles beyond Mile 188.

6 Groundhog Mountain

A split-rail fence and a rickety wooden observation tower overlook the lip of a grassy field that curves over a sky blue vista onto the Blue Ridge Mountains and Piedmont plateau. Flowering laurel and galax flurry over the greenery in white bursts, framing a picture perfect picnic spot. This, in any case, is the immediate impression you get on arriving at **Groundhog Mountain**, one of the more attractive parking overlooks on this stretch of the Blue Ridge Parkway. Note that the observation tower is built in the style of local historical tobacco barns.

A mile down the road is the log-and-daube **Puckett Cabin** (☎828-358-3400; www.nps.gov/blri; Mile 189.1, Blue Ridge Pkwy), last home of local midwife Orleana Hawks Puckett (1844–1939). The site of the property is dotted with exhibitions on the folkways and traditions of local mountain and valley folk.

The Drive ≫ Continue south for 24 miles to the Blue Ridge Music Center at Mile 213.

❼ Blue Ridge Music Center

As you approach the Tennessee border, you'll come across a large, grassy outdoor amphitheater. This is the **Blue Ridge Music Center** (☎276-236-5309; www.blueridgemusiccenter. net; 700 Foothills Rd/Mile 213, Blue Ridge Pkwy; ⏰10am-5pm late May-late Oct, 10am-5pm Thu-Mon early May-late May), an arts and music hub for the region that offers programming that focuses on local musicians carrying on the traditions of Appalachian music. Headline performances are mostly on weekends and but local musicians give free concerts on the breezeway of the visitor center most days from noon to 4pm. Bring a lawn chair and sit yourself down for an afternoon or evening performance. At night you can watch the fireflies glimmer in the darkness. There's a free 'Roots of American Music' exhibit on site too.

There are two trails in the vicinity – easy, flat **High Creek** (1.35 miles one-way) and moderate **Fisher Peak** loop (2.24 miles), which slopes up a small mountain peak.

The Drive ≫ Take VA-89 north for about 7 miles to reach downtown Galax. You'll pass working farms, some of which have quite the hardscrabble aesthetic – very different from the estate farms and stables of northern Virginia and the Shenandoah Valley.

TRIP HIGHLIGHT

❽ Galax (p78)

In Galax's historic downtown, look for the neon marquee of the **Rex Theater** (☎276-236-0329; www.rextheatergalax.com; 113 E Grayson St). This is a big old grande dame theater, with a Friday-night show called Blue Ridge Backroads (admission $5). Even if you can't make it to the theater at 8pm, you can listen to the two-hour show broadcast live to surrounding counties on 89.1 FM.

FIDDLE-DEE-DEE

Every second weekend in August for the last 70-odd years, Galax has hosted the **Old Fiddlers' Convention** (☎276-236-8541; www.oldfiddlersconvention.com; 601 S Main St, Felts Park), which now lasts for six days. Hosted by the local Loyal Order of the Moose Lodge, musicians come from all over to compete as well as to play. And for the record, this isn't just a fiddling competition; almost all of the instruments of the American roots music of the mountains are represented, including banjos, autoharp, dulcimer and dobro. Plus: there are clog dancing competitions. This fascinating local form of dance has roots that can be traced all the way back to the British Isles, and represents a relatively unbroken cultural thread that links the people of this region to their Scots-Irish ancestors.

Galax hosts the Smoke on the Mountain Barbecue Championship (www.smokeonthemountainva.com) on the second weekend in July. Teams from all over crowd the streets of downtown with their tricked-out mobile BBQ units.

If you think you've got what it takes to play, poke your head into Barr's Fiddle Shop (p79). This little music shop has a big selection of homemade and vintage fiddles and banjos along with mandolins, autoharps and harmonicas. You can get a lesson, or just admire the fine instruments that hang all over the walls.

The Drive >> Take US 221/US 58 east for 11 miles and hop on I-77 northbound. Take I-77 for 17 miles, then follow I-81 westbound for 65 miles to Abingdon.

TRIP HIGHLIGHT

❾ Abingdon (p79)

The gorgeous town of Abingdon anchors Virginia's southwesterly corner. Here, like a mirage in the desert, is the best hotel for hundreds of miles in any direction. The Martha Washington Inn (p80) resides inside a regal, gigantic brick mansion built for General Francis Preston in 1832. Pulling up after a long day's drive is like arriving at heaven's gates. You can almost hear the angels sing as you climb the grand stairs to the huge porch with views framed by columns.

The Barter Theatre (p81), across the street, is the big man on Main St in its historic red-brick building. This regional theater company puts on

its own productions of brand-name plays.

The Drive >> Take I-81 south from Abingdon for about 16 miles, then turn onto US 421 north/US 58 west; follow for about 20 miles to reach Hiltons.

❿ Carter Family Fold

Another star attraction is about 30 miles and a rural world away from Abingdon in the microscopic town of **Hiltons**, home of the musical Carter family. The Carters were one of several regional acts that recorded songs for the Victor Talking Machine Company during the 1927 Bristol Sessions. In the decades to follow, their ballads and old-time songs were broadcast on radio programs with an international reach, earning them acclaim far beyond southwest Virginia. Today, descendants of original band members AP, Sara and Maybelle Carter oversee the popular Saturday night old-time shows at the 900-person arena of the **Carter Family Fold** (✆276-386-6054; www.carterfamilyfold.org; 3449 AP Carter Hwy/SR 614; adult $10-15, 6-11yr $2; ⏰7:30pm Sat; ♿), which usualy include lively clog dancing. June Carter, daughter of Maybelle, performed with the family and later married

---

HISTORY OF MOUNTAIN MUSIC

A uniquely American genre, mountain music traces its roots to the earliest days of the country. European settlers brought their violins, also called fiddles, to the Virginia coast in the 1600s. Soon after, African slaves were creating music with their own banjo-like instruments. The fiddle and banjo eventually joined forces, and their combined sound migrated west. In the southern Appalachians, this fiddle-and-banjo music marinated with the songs and stories carried south from Pennsylvania by Scots-Irish and German immigrants, who established farms along the Great Wilderness Road in the mid-1700s. Today, mountain music is an umbrella term covering traditional old-time music and the more modern sounds of bluegrass.

DETOUR: DOLLYWOOD (P109)

Start: ⑪ Bristol

Across the Tennessee border, about two hours southwest of Bristol, is the legendary Dolly Parton's personal theme park **Dollywood** (☎865-428-9488; www. dollywood.com; 2700 Dollywood Parks Blvd, Pigeon Forge; adult/child $70/57; ☺mid-Mar–Dec, hours vary seasonally; [P][♿]). The Smoky Mountains come alive with lots of music and roller coasters. Fans will enjoy the daily Kinfolk Show starring Dolly's relatives or touring the two-story museum that houses her wigs, costumes and awards. You can buy your own coat of many colors in Dolly's Closet. To take this detour, take I-81 south for 75 miles, then take exit 407 and follow signs to Dollywood.

Johnny Cash. Cash's last public performance was at the Fold in 2003.

The Drive ≫ Come back the way you came on US 421/US 58 and drive about 20 miles to reach the Tennessee border and the town of Bristol.

---

⑪ Bristol

In nearby Bristol you can attend the **Bristol Motor Speedway** (☎423-989-6960; www.bristolmotor speedway.com; 151 Speedway Blvd; adult/senior/child $5/4/3; ☺tours 9am-4pm Mon-Sat year-round, 1-4pm Sun Feb-Oct), which runs lots of Nascar events. If they're not racing, you can still tour the 'world's fastest half-mile' and check out the 'Bristol Experience' in the adjacent museum.

Ready to head back home? Pop in one of the CDs you picked up along the way and trill to old-time music one last time as you ease back to modern life, keeping the wistful memories of banjos and bluegrass tucked safely inside your heart so nobody don't break it again.

Blue Ridge Parkway: North Carolina

4

This drive through the Tar Heel State on America's favorite byway curves through the High Country, climbs the East Coast's highest peak, then ends at the Smokies' doorstep.

TRIP HIGHLIGHTS

21 miles

Grandfather Mountain
Cross a mile-high suspension bridge for a parkway panorama

35 miles

Linville Falls
A family-friendly hike leads to views of a 90ft waterfall

START
Valle Crucis

5

6

Great Smoky Mountains National Park
FINISH
Waterrock Knob Visitor Center

10

11

Downtown Asheville
Enjoy indie shops and microbreweries

101 miles

Biltmore Estate
Peer at gargoyles, dumbwaiters and a bowling alley

109 miles

**5 DAYS
240 MILES/386KM**

GREAT FOR...

BEST TIME TO GO

May to October for leafy trees and seasonal attractions.

 ESSENTIAL PHOTO

The mile-high suspension bridge at Grandfather Mountain.

 BEST FOR FAMILIES

Enjoy a steam-train ride, gem mining, easy hiking and old-fashioned candy.

Grandfather Mountain Mile High Swinging Bridge (p46)

Blue Ridge Parkway: North Carolina

In North Carolina the parkway carves through a rugged landscape of craggy peaks, crashing waterfalls and thick forests, each languid curve unveiling another panorama of multi-hued trees and mist-shrouded mountains, with tantalizing viewpoints encouraging frequent stops. Mountain towns and beloved attractions like Grandfather Mountain add the right amount of pizzazz to the scenic mix.

1 Valle Crucis

How do you start a road trip through the mountains? With a good night's sleep and all the right gear, of course. You'll find both in Valle Crucis, a bucolic village 8 miles west of Boone. After slumbering beneath sumptuous linens at the 200-year-old Mast Farm Inn (p84), ease into the day sipping coffee in a rocking chair on the former farmhouse's front porch.

Down the road lies the **Original Mast General**

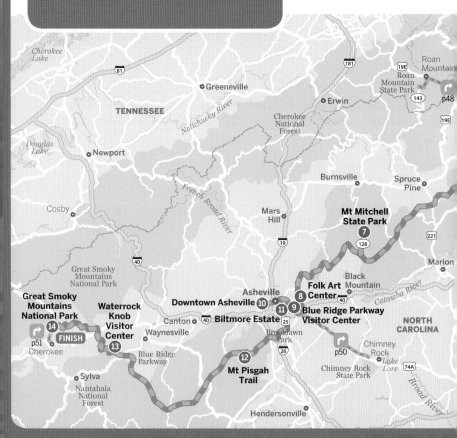

Store (☎828-963-6511; www.mastgeneralstore.com; 3565 Hwy 194 S, Valle Crucis; ⊙7am-6:30pm Mon-Sat, noon-6pm Sun; ♿). The first of the many Mast general stores that dot the High Country, this rambling clapboard building still sells many of the same products that it did back in 1883. As well as bacon, axes and hard candy, though, you'll now find hiking shoes, lava lamps and French country hand towels.

The store's annex (p85), just south along Hwy 194, sells outdoor apparel and hiking gear.

The Drive » Drive southeast on Hwy 194/Broadstone Rd, through 3 miles of rural splendor, then turn left at Hwy 105.

----

② Boone (p83)

If you're traveling with kids or are a wannabe prospector yourself, stop at **Foggy Mountain Gem Mine** (☎828-963-4367; www.foggymountaingems. com; 4416 Hwy 105 S; buckets $30-325; ⊙10am-5pm; ♿) to pan for semiprecious stones. Several gem-mining spots are located in these parts, but the graduate gemologists here take their craft a bit more seriously. Rough stones are sold by the bucketload, which you sift in a flume line. For additional fees, they'll cut and mount your favorite finds.

In downtown Boone, the bustling home of Appalachian State, you'll find quirky shopping and dining along **King St**, where Melanie's Food Fantasy (p84) is a good option for a hearty break-fast or tasty lunch. Keep an eye out for the bronze **statue** (642 W King St) of bluegrass legend Doc Watson, born nearby in 1923 and depicted strumming a Gallagher guitar on a street corner.

The Drive » From King St, turn onto Hwy 321 just past the Dan'l Boone Inn restaurant. Drive 4 miles then turn right at the Tweetsie Railroad theme park.

----

③ Blowing Rock (p85)

The parkway runs just above the village of Blowing Rock, which sits at an elevation of 4000ft. On a cloudy morning, drive south on Hwy 321 to the top of the mountain to check out the cloud-capped views of surrounding peaks. The eastern continental divide runs through the bar at the Green Park Inn (p86), a grand 1891 white-clapboard hotel. Author Margaret Mitchell stayed here while writing *Gone with the Wind*. For a memorable meal in a century-old lodge, call in at Bistro Roca (p86).

LINK YOUR TRIP

2 **Blue Ridge Parkway: Virginia**

Continue the ride into Virginia for pastoral landscapes, college towns and Dinosaur Kingdom II.

Riding the **Tweetsie Railroad** (☏828-264-9061; www.tweetsie.com; 300 Tweetsie Railroad Lane; adult/child 3-12yr $45/30; ☉9am-6pm Jun-late Aug, Fri-Sun mid-Apr–May, late Aug-Oct;), a 1917 coal-fired steam locomotive that chugs on a 3-mile loop past heroic cowboys and marauding Indians, is a rite of passage for every North Carolina child. It's the centerpiece of a theme park where Appalachian culture meets the Wild West, with midway rides, fudge shops and family-friendly shows to round out the fun.

The Drive ›› The entrance to the Blue Ridge Parkway is in Blowing Rock, 2.3 miles south of the Tweetsie Railroad. Once on the parkway, drive south 2 miles.

4 Moses H Cone Memorial Park

Hikers and equestrians share 25 miles of carriage roads on the former estate of Moses H Cone, a philanthropist and con-servationist who made his fortune in denim. Moses built a Colonial Revival mansion, Flat Top Manor, in 1901, which was given, along with the grounds, to the national park service in the 1950s. Directly accessible from the parkway at Mile 294, it now holds both a museum and the Parkway Craft Center (p86), where the Southern Highland Craft Guild sells superb Appalachian crafts at reasonable prices.

The Drive ›› Head south on the parkway, passing split rail fences, stone walls, streams and meadows. Just south of Mile 304, the parkway curves across the Linn Cove Viaduct, which, because of the fragility of the terrain, was the final section of the parkway to be completed, in 1987. Exit onto Hwy 221 at Mile 305, and drive 1 mile south.

TRIP HIGHLIGHT

5 Grandfather Mountain

The highest of the Blue Ridge Mountains, **Grand-father Mountain** (☏828-733-4337; www.grandfather.com; Mile 305, Blue Ridge Pkwy, Linville; adult/child 4-12yr $20/9; ☉8am-7pm Jun-Aug, 9am-5pm Mon-Fri, 9am-6pm Sat & Sun Mar, 9am-6pm Apr, May, Sep & Oct, 9am-5pm Nov-Feb; **P** ☖) looms north of the parkway 20 miles southwest of Blowing Rock. As a visitor destination, it's famous as the location of the **Mile High Swinging Bridge**, the focus of a privately owned attraction that also includes hiking trails plus a small museum and wildlife reserve. Don't let a fear of heights scare you away. Though the bridge

> ### LOCAL KNOWLEDGE: CREATING THE PARKWAY
>
> The construction of the Blue Ridge Parkway started in Virginia in 1935, during the Great Depression, when legions of unemployed young men were harnessed in the Civilian Conservation Corps, and set to work on the nation's infrastructure. By 1968 it was finished, but for 8 miles on the flanks of Grandfather Mountain in North Carolina, which were finally spanned when the Linn Cove Viaduct was completed in 1987.

Tweetsie Railroad

is a mile above sea level, and on gusty days you can hear its steel girders 'sing,' it spans a less fearsome chasm that's just 80ft deep.

Grandfather Mountain's loftiest summit, Calloway Peak (5946ft), is a strenuous 2.4-mile hike from the swinging bridge. Much of Grandfather Mountain is a Unesco Biosphere Reserve belonging to Grandfather Mountain State Park (www.ncparks.gov). Its 12 miles of wilderness hiking trails can also be accessed for free at Mile 300 on the parkway.

The Drive » Follow the parkway south and turn left just past Mile 316 to reach Linville Falls.

- - - - - - - - - - - - - - - -

TRIP HIGHLIGHT

⑥ Linville Falls

If you only have time for a single parkway hike, an hour-long sojourn at spectacular **Linville Falls** (☎828-765-1045; www.nps.gov/blri; Mile 316, Blue Ridge Pkwy, Linville; ☾trails 24hr, visitor center 9am-5pm Apr-Oct; Ⓟ ⓧ 🎁) makes a great option. Cross the Linville River from the parking lot, and head along **Erwin's View Trail**.

This moderate 1.6-mile round trip offers great close-up views of the river as it sweeps over two separate falls, before you climb a wooded hillside to enjoy magnificent long-range panoramas in two directions. One looks back to the falls, the other faces downstream, where the river crashes a further 2000ft through a rocky gorge. Swimming is forbidden at the falls.

The Drive » Drive south on the parkway and turn right, south of Mile 355, onto NC 128. Follow NC 128 into the park.

❼ Mt Mitchell State Park

Be warned: a major decision awaits visitors to North Carolina's first-ever **state park** (☎828-675-4611; www. ncparks.gov; 2388 Hwy 128; ⏰ park 7am-10pm May-Aug, closes earlier Sep-Apr, office 8am-5pm Apr-Oct, closed Sat & Sun Nov-Mar; **P**). Will you drive up Mt Mitchell, at 6684ft the highest peak east of the Mississippi, or will you hike to the top? Make your mind up at the park office, which sits beside a steep 2.2-mile summit trail that typically takes around 1½ hours one way.

Once up there, you'll see the grave of University of North Carolina

professor Elisha Mitchell. He came here in 1857 to prove his previous estimate of the mountain's height, only to fall from a waterfall and die. A circular ramp leads to dramatic views over and beyond the surrounding Black Mountains.

**The Drive ›› ** Return to the parkway and drive south to Mile 382. Look out for blooming rhododendrons during the last two weeks of June.

❽ Folk Art Center

Part gallery, part store, and wholly dedicated to Southern craftsmanship, the superb **Folk Art Center** (☎828-298-7928; www.southernhighlandguild. org; Mile 382, Blue Ridge Pkwy; ⏰9am-6pm Apr-Dec,

to 5pm Jan-Mar; **P**) is 6 miles east of downtown Asheville. The hand-crafted Appalachian chairs that hang above its lobby make an impressive appetizer for the permanent collection of the Southern Highland Craft Guild, a treasury of pottery, baskets, quilts and woodcarvings that's displayed on the 2nd floor. There are daily demonstrations by experts, and the Allanstand Craft Shop on the 1st floor sells high-quality traditional crafts.

**The Drive ›› ** Turn right onto the parkway and drive south. Cross the Swannanoa River and I-40, then continue to Mile 384.

DETOUR: ROAN MOUNTAIN STATE PARK, TENNESSEE

Start: ❺ **Grandfather Mountain**

The **Roan Mountain State Park** (☎reservations 800-250-8620, office 423-772-0190; http://tnstateparks.com/parks/about/roan-mountain; 1015 Hwy 143, Roan Mountain; ⏰8:30am-4pm; **P**) encompasses 2006 acres of southern Appalachian forest at the base of 6285ft Roan Mountain. On the top of Roan Mountain, straddling the Tennessee–North Carolina border, are the ruins of the old **Cloudland Hotel** site. The 300-room hotel was built in 1885 by Civil War general John T Wilder. Legend has it that North Carolinian sheriffs would hang out in the saloon, waiting for drinkers from the Tennessee side to stray across the line, as North Carolina was a dry state back then. The mountain top is also known for its bright purple-pink Catawba rhododendron blooms which burst forth in June. For hikers, there's a great 4.6-mile round-trip hike to Little Rock Knob (4918ft) through hardwood forests, with epic cliff-top views into Tennessee.

It's about 30 miles from Grandfather Mountain to the park. Follow the parkway south to US 221 S then follow the latter to Hwy 181 N. In Newland, pick up Hwy 194 N and drive to US 193E. Continue north to Roan Mountain, turning left onto Hwy 143 for the final push to the park.

⑨ Blue Ridge Parkway Visitor Center

At the Blue Ridge Parkway's helpful Asheville-area **visitor center** (☏828-348-3400; www.nps.gov/blri; Mile 384; ☺9am-5pm), you can sit back and let the scenery come to you, courtesy of a big-screen movie that captures the beauty and wonder of 'America's favorite journey.' Park rangers at the front desk gladly advise on parkway hiking trails, and sliding the digital panel across the amazing 'I-Wall' map brings up details of regional sites and activities. A separate desk is stocked with brochures and coupons for Asheville's attractions.

The Drive » Drive north, backtracking over the interstate and river, and exit at Tunnel Rd/Hwy 70. Drive west to Hwy 240, and follow it west to the exits for downtown Asheville.

TRIP HIGHLIGHT

⑩ Downtown Asheville (p86)

The undisputed 'capital' of the North Carolina mountains, Asheville is both a major tourist destination and one of the coolest small cities in the South. Home to an invigorating mix of hipsters, hippies and hikers, and offering easy access to outdoor adventures of all kinds, it's also a rare

MOUNTAIN MUSIC & BLUEGRASS VENUES

For locally grown fiddle-and-banjo music, grab your dance partner and head deep into the hills of the High Country. Regional shows and music jams are listed on the Blue Ridge Music Trails (www.blueridgemusicnc.com) and Blue Ridge National Heritage Area (www.blueridgeheritage.com) websites.

Here are three to get you started:

Mountain Home Music Concert Series (www.mountainhomemusic.com) Spring through fall, enjoy shows by Appalachian musicians in Boone on scheduled Saturday nights.

Isis Music Hall (www.isisasheville.com) Local bluegrass greats pop in at this Asheville institution's regular Tuesday-night session.

Historic Orchard at Altapass (www.altapassorchard.org) On weekends in May through October, settle in for an afternoon of music at Little Switzerland, Mile 328.

liberal enclave in the conservative countryside.

Strolling between downtown's historic art deco buildings, you'll encounter literary pilgrims celebrating the city's angsty famous son – and author of *Look Homeward, Angel* – at the Thomas Wolfe Memorial (p88); nostalgic gamers flipping the flippers at the Pinball Museum (p88); left-leaning intellectuals browsing at Malaprop's Bookstore & Cafe (p95); and design connoisseurs shopping for crafts in Horse & Hero (p94).

Head down the adjoining South Slope to find specialist microbreweries, such as spooky Burial (p92), which have earned

Asheville the nickname 'Beer City,' or hit the River Arts District to enjoy barbecue emporium 12 Bones (p91). Budget travelers looking to stay in Asheville should head for downtown's excellent Sweet Peas Hostel (p89).

The Drive » Follow Asheland Ave, which becomes McDowell St, south. After crossing the Swannanoa River, the entrance to the Biltmore Estate is on the right.

TRIP HIGHLIGHT

⑪ Biltmore Estate

The destination that put Asheville on the map, **Biltmore House** (☏800-411-3812; www.biltmore.com; 1 Approach Rd; adult/child 10-16yr $75/37.50; ☺house

9am-4:30pm, with seasonal variations; P), is the largest privately owned home in the US. Completed in 1895 for shipping and railroad heir George Washington Vanderbilt II, it was modeled after three châteaux that he'd seen in France's Loire Valley, and still belongs to his descendants. It's extraordinarily expensive to visit, but there's a lot to see; allow several hours to explore the entire 8000-acre Biltmore Estate. Self-guided tours of the house itself take in 39 points of interest, including our favorite, the two-lane bowling alley.

To hear the full story, pay $11 extra for an audio tour, or take the behind-the-scenes Upstairs Downstairs Tour ($20) or the more architecturally focused Rooftop Tour ($20). A 5-mile drive through the impeccably manicured estate, which also holds several cafes and two top-end hotels, leads to the winery and dairy farm in Antler Hill Village.

The Drive » Exit the grounds, then turn right onto Hwy 25 and continue for almost 3.5 miles to the parkway, and drive south.

DETOUR: CHIMNEY ROCK PARK

Start: ⑩ Downtown Asheville

The stupendous 315ft monolith known as Chimney Rock towers above the slender, forested valley of the Rocky Broad River, a gorgeous 28-mile drive southeast of Asheville on Hwy 74A. Protruding in naked splendor from soaring granite walls, its flat top bears the fluttering American flag. It's now the focus of a popular **state park** (☎800-277-9611; www. chimneyrockpark.com; Hwy 74A; adult/child 5-15yr $13/6; ⏰8:30am-7pm mid-Mar–Oct, 8:30am-6pm Nov, 10am-6pm Dec, 10am-6pm Fri-Tue Jan–mid-Mar; P). Climb the rock via the 499 steps of the Outcropping Trail or, assuming it's been repaired by the time you read this, simply ride the elevator deep inside the rock.

The leisurely and less crowded Hickory Nut Falls Trail leads in around 15 minutes through lush woods to the foot of a 404ft waterfall, high above the river. If it looks familiar, you may be remembering it from dramatic scenes in the *Last of the Mohicans,* filmed here.

Charming Chimney Rock village, immediately below the park, is a pleasant place to spend the night.

⑫ Mt Pisgah Trail

To enjoy an hour or two of hiking that culminate in a panoramic view, pull into the parking lot beside the **Mt Pisgah** trailhead, just beyond Mile 407. The 1.6-mile trail (one way) climbs to the mountain's 5721ft summit, topped by a lofty TV tower. The going gets steep and rocky in its final stretches, but you'll be rewarded with views of the French Broad River Valley as well as **Cold Mountain**, made famous by Charles Frazier's eponymous novel. One mile south you'll find a campground, a general store, a restaurant and an inn.

The Drive » The drive south passes the Graveyard Fields Overlook, where short trails lead to scenic waterfalls. From the 6047ft Richland Balsam Overlook at Mile 431.4 – the highest point on the parkway – continue south for another 20 miles.

⑬ Waterrock Knob Visitor Center

The Waterrock Knob Visitor Center (Mile 451.2) sits at an elevation of nearly 6000ft. With a four-state view, this scenic spot is a great place to see where you've been and to assess what lies ahead. Helpful signs identify the mountains along the far horizon.

The Drive » Continue on the parkway about 28 miles to

DETOUR:
MUSEUM OF THE CHEROKEE INDIAN

Start: ⑭ Great Smoky Mountains National Park

The best reason to visit Cherokee? The remarkable **Museum of the Cherokee Indian** (☏828-497-3481; www.cherokeemuseum.org; 589 Tsali Blvd/Hwy 441, at Drama Rd; adult/child 6-12yr $11/7; ⊙9am-7pm Jun-Aug, to 5pm Sep-May; [P]). This modern museum traces Cherokee history from their Paleo-Indian roots onwards. Its villain is the perfidious Andrew Jackson, who made his name fighting alongside the Cherokee but, as president, condemned them to the heartbreak of the Trail of Tears. One fascinating section follows the progress through 18th-century London of a Cherokee delegation that sailed to England in 1762.

the entrance to Great Smoky Mountains National Park at Mile 469.1.

---

⑭ Great Smoky Mountains National Park (p100)

Ah, the sweet reward at the end of this long and leafy trip: Great Smoky Mountains National Park. From the fog-choked summit of Clingmans Dome to the photogenic ghost town of Cades Cove to to the tinkling music of a dozen silvery waterfalls, there's something magical about this park and its mountains. Admission is free, so it's easy to continue your drive, but the park is best experienced by hiking its trails, sleeping in its remote campgrounds, splashing in its icy swimming holes and stepping into the historic cabins and churches.

Destinations

Virginia (p54)

Natural beauty, history, mountain music, wineries and craft breweries, Virginia's got it all.

North Carolina (p82)

During the day wear yourself out with the many outdoor adventures on offer, then relax with a beautiful meal and a craft beer at night.

North Carolina Blue Ridge Parkway
ANTHONY HEFLIN / SHUTTERSTOCK ©

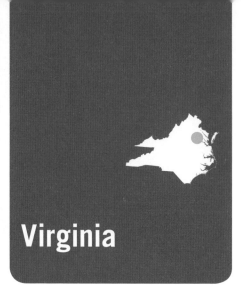

Virginia

Virginia combines stunning natural beauty, history and a vibrant mountain-music scene. Add to that top-quality tourist attractions, and you've got yourself a magnificent place for a road trip.

The commonwealth of Virginia is steeped in history and tradition. It's the birthplace of America, where English settlers established the first permanent colony in the New World in 1607. Since that time, the state has played a lead role in nearly every major American drama, from the Revolutionary and Civil Wars to the Civil Rights movement and the attacks of September 11, 2001.

Virginia's natural beauty is as diverse as its history and people. Chesapeake Bay and wide sandy beaches kiss the Atlantic Ocean. Pine forests, marshes and rolling green hills form the soft curves of the central Piedmont region, while the rolling Blue Ridge Mountains and stunning Shenandoah Valley line its back.

There's loads for the visitor to enjoy, including world-class tourist attractions such as Shenandoah National Park, a wealth of outdoor activities, a foot-tapping mountain-music scene and an ever-growing network of wine, beer and spirit trails to follow.

History

Humans have occupied Virginia for at least 5000 years. Several thousand Native Americans were already here in May 1607 when Captain James Smith and his crew sailed up Chesapeake Bay and founded Jamestown, the first permanent English colony in the New World. Named for Queen Elizabeth I – aka the 'Virgin Queen' – the territory originally occupied most of Amer-

ica's eastern seaboard. By 1610 most of the colonists had died from starvation in their quest for gold, until John Rolfe (husband of Pocahontas) discovered Virginia's real riches: tobacco.

A feudal aristocracy grew out of tobacco farming, and many gentry scions became Founding Fathers, including native son George Washington. In the 19th century, the slave-based plantation system grew both in size and incompatibility with the industrializing North; Virginia seceded in 1861 and became the epicenter of the Civil War. Following its defeat, the state walked a tense cultural tightrope, accruing a layered identity that included older aristocrats, a rural and urban working class, waves of immigrants and, today, the burgeoning tech-heavy suburbs of DC. The state revels in its history, yet still wants to pioneer the American experiment; thus, while Virginia reluctantly desegregated in the 1960s, today it houses one of the most ethnically diverse populations of the New South.

ⓘ Getting There & Away

The largest regional airports include **Washington Dulles International Airport** (IAD; www.metwashairports.com; ☎) in northern Virginia, **Richmond International Airport** (RIC; ☏ 804-226-3000; www.flyrichmond.com; 1 Richard E Byrd Terminal Dr; ☎) in Richmond, **Norfolk International Airport** (NIA; ☏ 757-857-3351; www.norfolkairport.com; 2200 Norview Ave; ☎)

Virginia State Capitol (p56), Richmond

in Norfolk, and Roanoke-Blacksburg Regional Airport (p77) in southwest Virginia. American, United and Delta serve **Charlottesville Albemarle Airport** (CHO; Map p67; ☏ 434-973-8342; www.gocho.com) in the Piedmont region.

Amtrak stops in Richmond at Main St Station (p62) and Staples Mill Rd Station (p62). There are also trains stations or platforms in Charlottesville (p65), Staunton (p71) and Roanoke (p77).

RICHMOND

☏ 804 / POP 223,170

Richmond has woken up from a very long nap – and we like it. The capital of the commonwealth of Virginia since 1780, and the capital of the Confederacy during the Civil War, it's long been an old-fashioned city clinging too tightly to its Southern roots. But an influx of new and creative young residents is energizing and modernizing the community.

Today the 'River City' shares a buzzing food-and-drink scene and an active arts community. The rough-and-tumble James River has also grabbed more of the spotlight, drawing outdoor adventurers to its rapids and trails. Richmond is also an undeniably handsome town that is easy to stroll, full of red-brick row houses, stately drives and leafy parks.

⦿ Sights

The three attractions that together comprise the American Civil War Museum (White House of the Confederacy, Historic Tredegar, and American Civil War Museum – Appomattox) can be visited on individual tickets, but it can often make sense to purchase a combination pass. Two of these are available: the Richmond Experience Package (adult/child six to 17 years $18/9), which gives entrance to the two Richmond attractions; and the Civil War Experience Package ($26/12), which gives entry to all three. Package tickets can be purchased online or at the individual site ticket offices.

★ **Virginia Museum of Fine Arts**   MUSEUM

(VMFA; ☏ 804-340-1405; www.vmfa.museum; 200 N Blvd, Museum District; ⊙ 10am-5pm Sat-Wed, to 9pm Thu & Fri) FREE Richmond is a cultured city, and this splendid art museum is the cornerstone of the local arts scene. Highlights of its eclectic, world-class collection include the Sydney and Frances Lewis Art Nouveau and Art Deco Galleries, which include furniture and decorative arts by designers including Eileen Gray, Josef Hoffmann and Charles Rennie Mackintosh. Other galleries house one of the largest Fabergé egg collections on display outside Russia, and American works by O'Keefe, Hopper, Henri, Whistler, Sargent and other big names.

Richmond

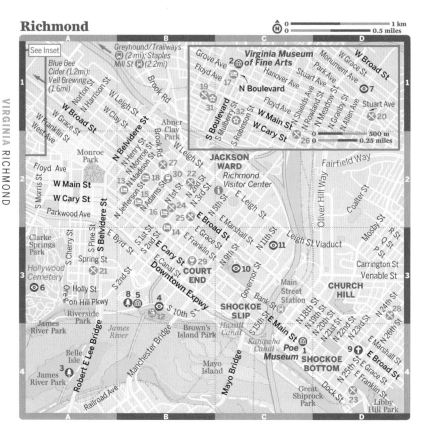

Poe Museum
MUSEUM

(☎804-648-5523; www.poemuseum.org; 1914-16 E Main St, Shockoe Bottom; adult/child 7-17yr $8/6; ⊙10am-5pm Tue-Sat, from 11am Sun) Contains the world's largest collection of manuscripts and memorabilia of poet and horror writer Edgar Allan Poe, who lived and worked in Richmond. Exhibits include the first printing of 'The Raven,' Poe's vest, his pen knife and a work chair with the back cut off – they say his boss at the *Southern Literary Messenger* wanted Poe to sit up straight. Pesky know-it-all. Stop by on the fourth Thursday of the month for the Poe-themed Unhappy Hour (6pm to 9pm April to October; $8).

Virginia State Capitol
NOTABLE BUILDING

(☎804-698-1788; www.virginiacapitol.gov; 1000 Bank St, Capitol Sq, Court End; ⊙9am-5pm Mon-Sat, from 1pm Sun) FREE Designed by Thomas Jefferson, the capitol building was completed in 1788 and houses the oldest legislative body in the Western Hemisphere – the Virginia General Assembly, established in 1619. Free one-hour guided tours of the historic building are available between 10am and 4pm Monday to Saturday, and between 1pm and 4pm on Sunday; a self-guided tour is also available. Temporary exhibits are staged in the underground galleries near the visitor entrance.

Canal Walk
WATERFRONT

(www.rvariverfront.com; btwn 5th & 17th Sts) The 1.25-mile waterfront Canal Walk between the James River and the Kanawha (ka-*naw*-wha) and Haxall Canals is a lovely way of seeing a dozen highlights of Richmond history in one go. There's also a pedestrian bridge across to Belle Isle (www.jamesriverpark.org; 300 Tredegar St), a scruffy but intriguing island in the James.

Richmond

Richmond National Battlefield Park PARK

(☏ 804-226-1981; www.nps.gov/rich; 470 Tredegar St; ⊙ battlefield sunrise-sunset, Civil War Visitor Center 9am-5pm) **FREE** The dozen Civil War sites and four visitor centers that comprise this park can be visited on an 80-mile driving tour around Richmond. The best place to begin the tour is at the **Civil War Visitor Center** housed in an old wool mill next to Historic Tredegar. Richmond was the capital of the Confederacy from 1861 to 1865, and at this center, which offers park maps, informative exhibits and an audiovisual presentation, you'll learn lots about the city's wartime story.

Historic Tredegar MUSEUM

(☏ 804-649-1861; https://acwm.org; 500 Tredegar St, Gambles Hill; adult/child 6-17yr $10/5; ⊙ 9am-5pm) Part of the multisite American Civil War Museum, this fascinating exhibit – housed inside an 1861 iron works that at its height employed 800 free and slave laborers – explores the causes and course of the Civil War from the Union, Confederate and African American perspectives.

St John's Episcopal Church CHURCH

(☏ 804-648-5015; www.historicstjohnschurch.org; 2401 E Broad St, Church Hill; tours adult/child 7-18yr $8/6; ⊙ 10am-4pm Mon-Sat, from 1pm Sun) It was here that firebrand Patrick Henry uttered his famous battle cry – 'Give me Liberty, or give me Death!' – during the rebellious 1775 Second Virginia Convention. The short but informative tour is given by guides dressed in period costume and traces the history of the church and of the famous speech. Above the pulpit, the rare 1741 sounding board and its sunburst are worth a closer look. Henry's speech is re-enacted at 1pm on Sundays in summer.

Hollywood Cemetery CEMETERY

(☏ 804-648-8501, tour reservations 804-649-0711; www.hollywoodcemetery.org; 412 S Cherry St, entrance cnr Albemarle & Cherry Sts; ⊙ 8am-6pm) **FREE** Perched above the James River rapids, this tranquil cemetery contains the gravesites of two US presidents (James Monroe and John Tyler), the only Confederate president (Jefferson Davis) and 18,000 Confederate soldiers. Guided walking tours are conducted at 10am Monday through Saturday from April to October, and Saturdays only in November (adult/child under 13 years $15/5). For a self-guided walk, check the virtual tour offered on the website.

White House of the Confederacy HISTORIC SITE

(☏ 804-649-1861; www.acwm.org; 1201 E Clay St, Court End; adult/child 6-17yr $12/6; ⊙ 10am-5pm) This 1818 building was the executive mansion of the Confederacy between 1861 and 1865, and the wartime home of its president, Jefferson Davis. Guided 45-minute tours of the interior explore the life of Davis, his family and the enslaved and free servants who worked in the house, offering plenty of quirky insights along the way (did you know the second-most powerful man in the Confederacy may have been a gay Jew?).

Monument Avenue
STREET

(btwn N Lombardy St & Roseneath Rd, Fan District) Famous southerners including JEB Stuart, Robert E Lee, Matthew Fontaine Maury, Jefferson Davis and Stonewall Jackson are memorialized in statue form along this beautiful tree-lined boulevard in northeast Richmond. The latest addition is a statue of African American tennis champion Arthur Ashe – heaven knows how he would have felt about being included in such company.

Snarky students at the nearby University of Richmond have been known to refer to the avenue's historic inhabitants as the 'largest collection of second place trophies in America.'

🏃 Activities

Riverside Outfitters
CANOEING

(☎ 804-560-0068; www.riversideoutfitters.net; Brown's Island, Downtown; per hr kayak/SUP boards/bike rental $15/15/10; ⊙9am-5pm Mon-Fri Nov-Mar, extended hr Apr-Oct) Rent a kayak, stand-up paddleboard or bike. The shop is on Brown's island across the street from Historic Tredegar (p57). These folks also offer guided rafting ($59 to $84) and kayaking ($59 to $69) trips, which launch from various locations.

🛏 Sleeping

★ HI Richmond
HOSTEL $

(☎ 804-729-5410; www.hiusa.org; 7 N 2nd St; dm $30-45, r $85-110, non-members add $3; ⊝❋�) 🧭 Inside the 1940s Otis Elevator Co building, this stylish and ecofriendly downtown option is one of the best hostels you'll ever encounter. Rooms and dorms are clean and bright, with lockers and charging stations; linen and towels are supplied. Communal facilities – free washing machines and dryers, lounge with pool table and TV, large and well-equipped kitchen – are excellent.

There's a book exchange and bike storage, free breakfast is provided, and the building is completely accessible for travelers with disabilities. Family rooms ($105 to $160) are also available.

Graduate
BOUTIQUE HOTEL $$

(☎ 804-644-9871; www.graduatehotels.com/richmond; 301 W Franklin St; r from $139; P❋�🐾) The Richmond branch of a popular budget boutique chain, this hip hotel has a cafe on the ground floor, a seasonal bar on the rooftop and spacious rooms with an attractive decor and good amenities. Sadly, the hotel's internet service is really slow.

Museum District B&B
B&B $$

(☎ 804-359-2332; www.museumdistrictbb.com; 2811 Grove Ave, Museum District; r $155-175; P⊝❋�) On a leafy boulevard that also houses the Virginia Museum of Fine Arts, this stately 1920s brick B&B has earned many admirers for its warm welcome. Rooms are comfortably set and guests can enjoy the wide front porch, cozy parlor with fireplace, and generous cooked breakfasts – plus wine and cheese in the evenings. It's near the dining and drinking of Carytown.

Linden Row Inn
HOTEL $$

(☎ 804-783-7000; www.lindenrowinn.com; 100 E Franklin St; r from $139, ste $289; P❋@�) This antebellum gem has 70 attractive rooms (with period Victorian furnishings) spread among neighboring Greek Revival town houses in an excellent downtown location. Friendly Southern hospitality, reasonable prices and thoughtful extras (free passes to the YMCA, free around-town shuttle service) sweeten the deal. There'a also an on-site cafe.

★ Quirk Hotel
BOUTIQUE HOTEL $$$

(☎ 804-340-6040; www.destinationhotels.com/quirk-hotel; 201 W Broad St, Monroe Ward; r $170-450, ste $330-680; P⊝❋�🐾) From the moment you stroll into the big-windowed lobby, which houses a glam bar and restaurant, this downtown boutique choice impresses. The high ceilings and maple floors in rooms are a direct link to the building's past life as a luxury department store. Beds, bathrooms and amenities are excellent. The hotel's popular rooftop bar is open late April to late October.

Jefferson Hotel
HISTORIC HOTEL $$$

(☎ 804-649-4750; www.jeffersonhotel.com; 101 W Franklin St; r from $315; P⊝❋�🏊🐾) The vision of tobacco tycoon and Confederate major Lewis Ginter, this beaux arts–style hotel was completed in 1895. Rooms sport an old-fashioned but inviting decor and are

PHOTO BY DEB LINDSEY FOR THE WASHINGTON POST VIA GETTY IMAGES

Veil Brewing (p61), Richmond

extremely comfortable; amenities and facilities are good. According to rumor (probably untrue), the magnificent grand staircase in the lobby served as the model for the famed stairs in *Gone with the Wind*.

Even if you don't stay here, it's worth having a peek inside. Pick up a hotel walking-tour brochure at the concierge desk. A statue of the hotel's namesake, Thomas Jefferson, anchors the lobby. Afternoon tea is served beneath Tiffany stained glass in the Palm Court lobby (from 3pm Friday to Sunday), and cocktails are shaken or stirred at the grand Lemaire Bar.

Eating

Stoplight Gelato ICE CREAM

(☎804-664-9400; www.stoplightgelatocafe.com; 405 Brook Rd, Jackson Ward; 1 scoop $1.75; ⏲8am-9:30pm Wed-Mon) Jackson Ward's favorite ice cream shop keeps the local community happy with gelato, soft-serve ice cream, sundaes, floats, sodas, milkshakes and smoothies.

★**Perly's** DELI $

(☎804-912-1560; www.perlysrichmond.com; 111 E Grace St, Monroe Ward; brunch dishes $7-14, sandwiches $9-13; ⏲8am-9pm Mon-Sat, to 3pm Sun) Generations of locals have enjoyed Yiddish specialties at Perly's (it dates from 1962) and we think you should too. Choose from treats including corned beef hash, cinnamon babka, knish and latkes at brunch (which runs till 3pm daily) and opt for one of the sandwiches at lunch. There's booth and bar seating, and a friendly retro vibe.

★**Sugar & Twine** CAFE $

(☎804-204-1755; www.sugartwine.com; 2928 W Cary St, Carytown; pastries $2-3, sandwiches $5-6; ⏲7am-8pm Mon-Sat, to 6pm Sun; 📶🌿) Let's face it: contemporary coffee culture hasn't made inroads in Virginia yet. Fortunately, stylish cafes like this one are in the vanguard. We like everything about Sugar & Twine: the excellent espresso coffee, delicious pastries, tasty sandwiches (some vegan and veggie; gluten-free bread available), free wi-fi and friendly staff.

Kuba Kuba CUBAN $

(☎804-355-8817; www.kubakuba.info; 1601 Park Ave, Fan District; sandwiches $8-10, mains $13-20; ⏲9am-9:30pm Mon-Thu, to 10pm Fri & Sat, to 8pm Sun; 🌿) Kuba Kuba feels like a bodega straight out of Old Havana, with mouth-watering roast pork dishes, Spanish-style omelets and panini offered at rock-bottom prices. Finish with a dessert and good espresso coffee.

Sub Rosa BAKERY $

(☎804-788-7672; www.subrosabakery.com; 620 N 25th St, Church Hill; pastries $1.25-4.50; ⏲7am-6pm Tue-Fri, 8am-5pm Sat & Sun) In the residential Church Hill neighborhood, this wood-fired bakery serves some of the best baked goods in the south. Some of the treats on offer are Turkish – flakey *börek* stuffed with cheese, meat or greens and

VINEYARDS OF VIRGINIA

Home to more than 200 vineyards, Virginia has a rising presence in the wine world. Good places to begin an investigation of the local scene lie just outside of DC in Loudon County, and designated wine trails continue throughout the state. For maps, wine routes and loads of other viticultural info, visit www.virginiawine.org.

It's a hard task to nominate only a few wineries as highlights, but here's our best shot.

Loudoun Country

Bluemont Vineyard (☑540-554-8439; www.bluemontvineyard.com; 18755 Foggy Bottom Rd, Bluemont; tastings $15; ⊙11am-6pm Sat-Thu, to 8pm Fri, reduced hr winter; 🐾)

Breaux Vineyards (☑540-668-6299; www.breauxvineyards.com; 36888 Breaux Vineyards Lane, Hillsboro; tastings $15; ⊙11am-6pm mid-Mar–Oct, to 5pm Nov-early Mar; 🐾)

Sunset Hills Vineyard (☑540-882-4560; www.sunsethillsvineyard.com; 38295 Fremont Overlook Lane, Purcellville; tastings $10; ⊙noon-5pm Mon-Thu, to 6pm Fri, 11am-6pm Sat & Sun; Ⓟ)✎

Tarara Vineyard (☑703-771-7100; www.tarara.com; 13648 Tarara Lane; tastings $10-20; ⊙11am-5pm Mon-Thu, to 6pm Fri-Sun, closed Tue & Wed Nov-Mar; 🐾)

Also see loudounfarms.org/craft-beverages/wine-trail and www.visitloudoun.org/things-to-do/wine-country.

Blue Ridge Parkway

Chateau Morrisette (p78)

Also see www.mountainroadwineexperience.com.

The Piedmont

Barboursville Vineyards (Map p67; ☑540-832-3824; www.bbv.wine.com; 17655 Winery Rd; tastings $7; ⊙tasting room 10am-5pm Mon-Sat, from 11am Sun)

Grace Estate (Map p67; ☑434-823-1486; www.graceestatewinery.com; 5273 Mount Juliet Farm, Crozet; tasting $9; ⊙11am-5:30pm Wed, Thu & Sun, to 9pm Fri & Sat)

King Family Vineyards (Map p67; ☑434-823-7800; www.kingfamilyvineyards.com; 6550 Roseland Farm, Crozet; tastings $10, tour $20; ⊙10am-5:30pm Thu-Tue, to 8:30pm Wed; 🐾)

Pippin Hill (p65)

Also see www.americaswinecountry.com and https://monticellowinetrail.com.

---

sweet *poğaça* (buns). Make your choice at the counter and enjoy it with a well-made coffee or Moroccan mint tea. Indoor and outdoor seating.

Mama J's　　　　　　　　　AMERICAN $
(☑804-225-7449; www.mamajskitchen.com; 415 N 1st St, Jackson Ward; mains $8-15, sandwiches $5-9; ⊙11am-9pm Sun-Thu, to 10pm Fri & Sat) The fried catfish may not look fancy, but it sure tastes like heaven. Set in the historic African American neighborhood of Jackson Ward, Mama J's serves delicious fried chicken and legendary fried catfish, along with collard greens, mac 'n' cheese, candied yams and other fixings. The service is friendly and the lines are long. Come early to beat the crowds.

Sidewalk Cafe　　　　AMERICAN, GREEK $
(☑804-358-0645; www.sidewalkinthefan.com; 2101 W Main St, Fan District; mains $11-18, sandwiches $9-10, brunch dishes $8-13; ⊙11am-2am Mon-Fri, from 9:30am Sat & Sun) A much-loved local haunt, Sidewalk Cafe feels like a dive bar (year-round Christmas lights, wood-paneled walls, kitschy artwork), but the food is first-rate. There are outdoor seating on the sidewalk, daily specials (eg Taco Tuesdays) and legendary weekend brunches.

Rappahannock Oyster Saloon　　SEAFOOD $$
(☑804-545-0565; www.rroysters.com; 320 E Grace St, Monroe Ward; oyster in half shell $2.25; ⊙11:30am-11pm Mon-Thu, 11:30am-midnight Fri, 3pm-midnight Sat, 3-11pm Sun) One of the least salty oysters on the East Coast, the Rappa-

hannock ('Rapp') is a smooth and sweet mollusc beloved in Virginia. This is a great place to try it, whether it be raw with a wedge of lemon on the side, enlivened with watermelon tequila granita and trout caviar, or served Rockefeller style (topped with butter, green herbs, and bread crumbs and broiled till golden).

Daily Kitchen & Bar   MODERN AMERICAN $$
(☑804-342-8990; www.thedailykitchenandbar.com; 2934 W Cary St, Carytown; lunch mains $9-16, dinner mains $12-26; ⊙7am-10pm Sun-Thu, to midnight Fri & Sat; 🖋) 🌱 In the heart of Carytown, the Daily is a great dining and drinking choice no matter the time of day. Stop by for lump crab omelets at breakfast, blackened mahi-mahi BLT at lunch and seared scallops by night. Extensive vegan options, first-rate cocktails, a buzzing dining room and expansive terrace all seal the deal.

Millie's Diner   MODERN AMERICAN $$
(☑804-643-5512; www.milliesdiner.com; 2603 E Main St; lunch mains $9-14, dinner mains $16-29; ⊙11am-2:30pm & 5:30-10:30pm Tue-Fri, 9am-3pm & 5:30-10:30pm Sat, 9am-3pm Sun) Lunch, dinner or weekend brunch – Richmond icon Millie's does it all, and does it well. It's a small, but handsomely designed space with creative seasonal fare. The Devil's Mess – an open-faced omelet with spicy sausage, curry, veg, cheese and avocado – is legendary.

★L'Opossum   AMERICAN, FRENCH $$$
(☑804-918-6028; www.lopossum.com; 626 China St, Oregon Hill; mains $22-36; ⊙5pm-midnight Tue-Sat) We're not exactly sure what's going on at this gastronomic laboratory, but it works. The name of the place is terrible. And dishes come with names that are self-consciously hip and verging on offensive ('Vegan Orgy on Texan Beach'). What ties it together? The culinary prowess of award-winning chef David Shannon and his attentive and talented staff.

Make a reservation or get here early to snag a seat at the bar.

🍷 Drinking & Nightlife

New craft breweries and a cider house or two are bringing lively crowds to the rapidly developing Scott's Addition neighborhood north of Broad St. For a full list of breweries across the city and their locations, check out the map for the **Richmond Beer Trail** (www.visitrichmondva.com/drink/richmond-beer-trail). Neighborhood pubs are the draw in the Fan and Carytown districts, just west of downtown.

Blue Bee Cider   DISTILLERY
(☑804-231-0280; www.bluebeecider.com; 1320 Summit Ave, Scott's Addition; ⊙1-8pm Mon-Fri, noon-9pm Sat, to 7pm Sun) Stop in for a taste of a rotating list of top-notch, small-batch ciders. Recipes range from crisp, apples-only varieties to berry- or hop-infused blends. Blue Bee often collaborates with other local distillers and brewers – the sweet and spicy Firecracker, made with a ginger *eau de vie* from Catoctin Creek Distilling Co, is a standout example.

Ample outdoor seating makes Blue Bee a summer afternoon hotspot.

Answer Brewpub   MICROBREWERY
(☑804-282-1248; http://theanswerbrewpub.com; 6008 W Broad St; ⊙4pm-midnight Mon-Wed, noon-midnight Thu-Sat, noon-10pm Sun) Killer IPAs, very strange fruited sours (a cross between tart beer and fruit smoothie) and a hip Asian nightclub vibe make this brewpub one of the most unusual and popular drinking dens in Richmond. There are 56 taps, two bars, and a stage area for live music.

Veil Brewing   MICROBREWERY
(www.theveilbrewing.com; 1301 Roseneath Rd, Scott's Addition; ⊙4-9pm Tue-Thu, to 10pm Fri, noon-10pm Sat, noon-6pm Sun) One of the most popular craft breweries in the emerging Scott's Addition neighborhood, Veil is known for its hop-forward beers, plenty of which are offered on draft at the taproom.

Saison   BAR
(☑804-269-3689; www.saisonrva.com; 23 W Marshall St, Jackson Ward; ⊙5pm-2am) This hipster hole-in-the-wall is a peculiar mash up of wine bar, cafe and restaurant. Creative cocktails, craft beer and local wines are on offer, as is a menu of small plates (many vegetarian), burgers and fried chicken. We recommend heading here for drinks rather than meals.

Capital Ale House   BAR
(☑804-780-2537; www.capitalalehouse.com; 623 E Main St, Court End; ⊙11am-1:30am Mon-Fri, from 10am Sat & Sun) Popular with political wonks from the nearby state capitol, this downtown pub has a superb beer selection (more than 40 on tap and 140 bottled) and decent food. Regular live gigs are staged in the music hall.

⭐ Entertainment

Cary Street Cafe   LIVE MUSIC
(☏ 804-353-7445; www.carystreetcafe.com; 2631 W Cary St, Carytown; ⏱ 11am-2am) Live music (plus the odd karaoke crooner) emanates from this excellent bar just about every night of the week. This spot is proudly pro-hippie, but doesn't just bust hippie tunes; the gigs juke from reggae and folk to alt-country and gypsy rock. On Sunday afternoons, old-time jazz takes center stage.

Byrd Theater   CINEMA
(☏ 804-353-9911; www.byrdtheatre.com; 2908 W Cary St, Carytown; tickets from $4) You can't beat the price at this classic 1928 cinema, which shows second-run films and longtime favorites. Wurlitzer-organ concerts precede the Saturday-night shows.

ℹ Information

Richmond Visitor Center (☏ 804-783-7450; www.visitrichmondva.com; 405 N 3rd St; ⏱ 9am-5pm; 📶)

ℹ Getting There & Away

Amtrak (www.amtrak.com) trains stop at the **Staples Mill Rd station** (www.amtrak.com; 7519 Staples Mill Rd), 7 miles north of town (accessible to downtown via bus 27). More-convenient but less-frequent trains stop downtown at the **Main St Station** (www.amtrak.com; 1500 E Main St). Richmond is serviced by the Northeast Regional, Carolinian, Palmetto, Silver Star and Silver Meteor lines, all of which link the city frequently with Washington, DC (tickets from $28, 2¼ to 2½ hr).
Greyhound/Trailways Bus Station (☏ 804-254-5910; www.greyhound.com; 2910 North Blvd, The Diamond; ⏱ 24hr)

ℹ Getting Around

Street parking costs $1.25 per hour.

CHARLOTTESVILLE

📋 434 / POP 46,910
Set in the shadow of the Blue Ridge Mountains, Charlottesville is regularly ranked as one of the country's best places to live. This culturally rich town is home to the architecturally resplendent University of Virginia (UVA), which attracts Southern aristocracy and artsy lefties in equal proportions. The UVA grounds, Main St and the pedestrian downtown mall area overflow with students, professors and visiting tourists, endowing 'C-ville' with a lively, cultured and diverse atmosphere.

⊙ Sights

⭐ **University of Virginia**   UNIVERSITY
(☏ 434-924-0311; www.virginia.edu) Thomas Jefferson founded the University of Virginia, and designed what he called an 'Academical Village' embodying the spirit of communal living and learning. At the heart of this 'village' is the Lawn, a large gently sloping

Rotunda, Charlottesville

grassed field fringed by columned pavilions, student rooms, the Standford White–designed Old Cabell Hall (1898) and Jefferson's famous Rotunda, modelled on Rome's Pantheon. Together, the original Neoclassical and Palladian-style university buildings and Jefferson's Monticello comprise a Unesco World Heritage Site.

Rotunda   NOTABLE BUILDING
(☑434-924-7969; www.rotunda.virginia.edu; 1826 University Ave; ⊙9am-5pm) The centerpiece of UVA is the Jefferson-designed Rotunda, modelled after Rome's Pantheon and constructed between 1822 and 1832. It has always functioned as a library. Free guided tours (www.uvaguides.org) of the original university and lawn area are offered daily at 10am, 11am and 2pm during the school year (September to April) and start in the Rotunda.

🛏 Sleeping

Fairhaven   GUESTHOUSE $
(☑434-933-2471; www.fairhavencville.com; 413 Fairway Ave; r $55-90; 🅿❄🛜🐾) This friendly and welcoming guesthouse is a great deal if you don't mind sharing facilities (there's just one bathroom for the three rooms). Each room has wood floors, comfy beds and a cheerful color scheme, and guests can use the kitchen, living room and backyard. It's about a 1-mile walk to the pedestrian mall.

⭐ **Residence Inn by Marriott**   HOTEL $$
(☑434-220-0075; www.marriott.com; 315 W Main St; studio $149-299, 1-bed apt $189-399, 2-bed apt $229-499; 🅿♿❄🛜🏊🐾) We're not usually chain-hotel fans, but this excellent place deserves serious praise. Its location couldn't be better, and its clean, comfortable and well-equipped studios and apartments make a great base for a Charlottesville stay. Facilities include a pool, bar, gym, and coin-operated laundry, and there's even a free shuttle service within a 10-mile radius (including the airport).

⭐ **South Street Inn**   B&B $$
(☑434-979-0200; www.southstreetinn.com; 200 W South St; r $135-325, ste $195-355; 🅿❄🛜) Having gone through previous incarnations as a girls' finishing school, a boarding house and a brothel, this elegant 1856 building, with its picture-perfect front porch, now houses a heritage-style B&B with 11 well-sized and beautifully presented rooms. There are extra rooms in an attached cottage. Breakfast

DON'T MISS

MONTICELLO

The house at Monticello (☑434-984-9800; www.monticello.org; 931 Thomas Jefferson Pkwy; adult/child 5-11yr $22/9; ⊙8:30am-6pm Mon-Fri, to 7pm Sat & Sun, hr vary seasonally) is an architectural masterpiece designed and inhabited by Thomas Jefferson, Founding Father and third US president, who spent 40 years building his dream home. It was finally completed in 1809. Today it is the only home in America designated a Unesco World Heritage Site. The centerpiece of a plantation that once covered 5000 acres, it can be visited on guided tours (ground floor only) and its grounds and outbuildings can be explored in themed and self-guided tours.

is served in the library, as is complimentary wine and cheese every evening.

🍴 Eating

⭐ **Bodo's Bagels**   BAGELS $
(☑434-293-6021; www.bodosbagels.com; 1609 University Ave; bagels $0.80-4; ⊙7am-8pm Mon-Fri, 8am-4pm Sat & Sun) Students and university staff are regulars at this Charlottesville institution, lured by its wonderful bagels and its location on UVA Corner. Choose from a large array of options (plain, slathered with butter or cream cheese, topped with egg). Also offers sandwiches. Eat in or order to go.

Mudhouse Coffee Roasters   CAFE $
(☑434-984-6833; www.mudhouse.com; 213 W Main St; pastry $3; ⊙7am-10pm Mon-Thu, to 11pm Fri & Sat, to 7pm Sun; 🛜) Its mantra is 'Beautiful coffee. Thoughtfully sourced. Carefully roasted.' and we can attest to the fact that this cafe on the pedestrian mall practices what it preaches. Excellent coffee (espresso and drip) and delicious pastries are enjoyed in stylish surrounds or at tables on the mall.

Citizen Burger   AMERICAN $
(☑434-979-9944; www.citizenburgerbar.com; 212 E Main St; burgers $7-21; ⊙11:30am-10:30pm Sun-Thu, to 11:30pm Fri & Sat; 🍴) 🌿 The ethos at this hugely popular burger joint on the pedestrian mall is commendably local and sustainable (organically raised, grass-fed cows, Virginia-made cheeses and beers). Don't

Charlottesville

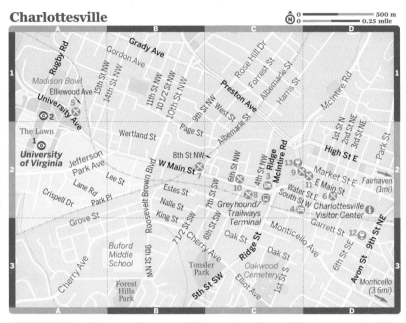

Charlottesville

miss the truffle fries. The bar stays open after meal service finishes.

Spot   VEGAN, VEGETARIAN **$**
(☎434-465-1267; www.vunoodles.com/the-spot.html; 110 2nd St NW; mains $8-10; ⏱11am-2pm Mon-Fri Mar-Dec; 🖉) Its somewhat scruffy appearance doesn't put off local students, who flock to this lounge-room-style eatery just off the pedestrian mall. Serving a solely vegetarian and vegan menu, its most popular item is the vegan BBQ and slaw on naan bread with a cilantro-lime dressing, but both the banh mi and salad bowl with curried tofu also have fans.

Feast!   AMERICAN **$**
(☎434-244-7800; www.feastvirginia.com; 416 W Main St; mains $8-10; ⏱10am-7pm Mon-Fri, 9am-6pm Sat) Inside the Main Street Market, this gourmet grocer is a fine spot to load up on picnic fare, with wines, a wonderfully smelly array of cheeses, fruits and other temptations. Its cafe serves fresh sandwiches (made to order from 11am to 3pm), soups, and salads.

⭐**Oakhart Social**   MODERN AMERICAN **$$**
(☎434-995-5449; www.oakhartsocial.com; 511 W Main St; small plates $8-14, pizza $15; ⏱5pm-midnight Tue-Sun, to 2am Fri & Sat) Seasonally inspired small plates and wood-fired piz-

VIRGINIA CHARLOTTESVILLE

zas emerge from the kitchen of this hipster haunt at a great rate, keeping its loyal crew of regulars fed and happy. On warm nights, the front patio is a perfect cocktail-sipping spot, and the bar is a great spot for solo diners.

Continental Divide MEXICAN $$
(☑ 434-984-0143; www.eatdivide.com; 811 W Main St; mains $9-17; ⊗ 5-10pm Mon, to 10:15pm Tue-Thu, to 10:45pm Fri & Sat, to 9:45pm Sun) This fun, easy-going spot has no sign (look for the neon 'Get in Here' in the window) but is well worth seeking out for its Mexican fusion fare and to knock back one of Charlotteville's best margaritas.

★ **Public Fish & Oyster** SEAFOOD $$$
(☑ 434-995-5542; www.publicfo.com; 513 W Main St; mains $19-26; ⊗ 4-9pm Sun & Mon, to 9:30pm Tue-Thu, to 10pm Fri & Sat) This bright and inviting space will catch your eye, but it's the skillfully seasoned seafood dishes that will keep you inside ordering plate after plate of freshly shucked oysters, mussels and other maritime delights. If you're a raw oyster virgin, this is the place to change that story. The twice-cooked Belgian fries with sea salt are fantastic. Great service too.

🍷 Drinking & Nightlife

At night, the bars along University Ave attract students and 20-somethings. Charlottesville is the kick-off point for the craft breweries along the Brew Ridge Trail (www. brewridgetrail.com).

★ **Blue Mountain Brewery** BREWERY
(Map p67; ☑ 540-456-8020; www.bluemountain brewery.com; 9519 Critzer's Shop Rd, Afton; ⊗ 11am-10pm Mon-Sat, to 9pm Sun) Located 20 miles from Charlottesville near the gorgeous high slopes of Skyline Drive, Blue Mountain Brewery is some kind of wonderful. These people are dedicated to their craft and their craft beers, which includes a crisp Bavarian-style wheat beer that is good in the hot summer swelter, and the muscular Full Nelson, brewed with local hops. Great food (pizzas, burgers, sandwiches) too.

Pippin Hill WINERY
(☑ 434-202-8063; www.pippinhillfarm.com; 5022 Plank Rd, North Garden; tastings $10; ⊗ 11am-5pm Sun & Tue-Fri, to 4:30pm Sat) 🍃 Wonderful views over the rolling plateau of the Piedmont await you at this exemplar of sustainable viticulture. The restaurant has

an unapologetically locovore philosophy, and the results are inspired – enjoy them over lunch in the tasting room or learn how to emulate them by attending one of the regular cooking classes. The wines are well regarded too – try the viognier or cabernet sauvignon.

Champion Brewing Company BREWERY
(☑ 434-326-3859; www.championbrewingcompa ny.com; 324 6th St SE; ⊗ 5-9pm Mon-Wed, 4-11pm Thu, 1-11pm Fri & Sat, 1-9pm Sun) The Champion is in Charlottesville proper, so there's no need to worry about calling that cab after your brewery-bound tasting test. More importantly, these people know their stuff, as evidenced by their heavy porters and flavorful kolsches. There's occasional live music. Find it in an industrial enclave off Garrett St.

Whiskey Jar COCKTAIL BAR
(☑ 434-202-1549; www.thewhiskeyjarcville.com; 227 W Main St; lunch mains $10-15, dinner mains $12-32; ⊗ 11am-midnight Mon-Thu, to 2am Fri & Sat, 11am-3pm Sun) On the pedestrian mall, Whiskey Jar offers a huge (more than 125 varieties!) whiskey selection in a rustically hip setting – wooden furniture with waitstaff wearing plaid and drinks in mason jars. Also serves neo-Southern comfort food, including great barbecue.

ℹ Information

Charlottesville Visitor Center (☑ 434-293-6789; www.visitcharlottesville.org; 610 E Main St; ⊗ 9am-5pm) Located above the city's transit station, at the eastern end of the pedestrian mall; sells various block passes for area attractions and has restrooms. For the mall location, you can park in the Market St and Water St garages and the visitor center will validate two hours.

ℹ Getting There & Away

Amtrak (www.amtrak.com; 810 W Main St; ⊗ ticket office 6am-9:30pm) Two daily trains to Washington, DC (from $27, 2¾ hours).

Charlottesville Albemarle Airport (p55) Located 10 miles north of downtown; offers nonstop flights along the East Coast and to Chicago.

Greyhound/Trailways Terminal (☑ 434-295-5131; www.greyhound.com; 310 W Main St; ⊗ ticket office 8am-10pm) Runs two daily buses to Richmond (from $13, 1¼ hours), three to Roanoke (from $18, 2½ hours) and two to Washington, DC (from $18, three hours).

SHENANDOAH VALLEY

VIRGINIA SHENANDOAH NATIONAL PARK

Local lore says Shenandoah was named for a Native American word meaning 'Daughter of the Stars.' True or not, there's no question this is God's country, and one of the most beautiful places in America. The 200-mile-long valley and its Blue Ridge Mountains are packed with picturesque small towns, wineries, microbreweries, preserved battlefields and caverns. This was once the western border of colonial America, settled by Scots-Irish frontiersmen who were Highland Clearance refugees. Outdoor activities such as hiking, cycling, camping, fishing, horseback riding and canoeing abound, and hitting the road on the famed Skyline Drive is an unforgettable experience, particularly in the fall when the palette of the forest canopy ranges from russet red to copper-tinged orange.

❶ Getting There & Away

The best way to explore is by car. The I-81 and I-64 are the primary interstates here. The largest airport is Roanoke-Blacksburg Regional Airport (p77). Amtrak stops at the train station (p71) in Staunton and the Virginia Breeze (p69) bus service to/from Washington, DC, stops at Arlington, Front Royal, Staunton and Lexington (tickets $15 to $50).

Shenandoah National Park

One of the most spectacular national parks in the country, Shenandoah (☑ 540-999-3500; www.nps.gov/shen; Skyline Dr; 1-week pass per car $25; ☉ year-round) is like a new smile from nature: in spring and summer the wildflowers explode, in fall the leaves burn bright red and orange, and in winter a cold, starkly beautiful hibernation period sets in. White-tailed deer are a common sight and, if you're lucky, you might spot a black bear, bobcat or wild turkey. The park lies just 75 miles west of Washington, DC. With the famous 105-mile Skyline Drive and more than 500 miles of hiking trails, including 101 miles of the Appalachian Trail, there is plenty to do and see.

The park is open year-round although Skyline Drive may close during bad weather. Leashed pets are allowed at campgrounds and pet-friendly lodgings and on most trails, but the leash must be no longer than 6ft.

◉ Sights & Activities

Hawksbill (4050ft; p22) is the highest peak in the park and a well-known nesting area for peregrine falcons. Stand on the rustic stone observation platform atop the peak for long-lasting impressions of the park's wondrous beauty.

Old Rag Mountain HIKING
(www.nps.gov/shen; Rte 600) One of the best day hikes in the state, this extremely tough, full-day 9.2-mile circuit trail culminates in an adventurous rocky scramble – one that's suitable only for the physically fit. Your reward is the summit of Old Rag Mountain, not to mention the fantastic views along the way.

The most commonly used trailhead is accessed from outside the park. From Madison, follow US 29 north for 12.8 miles then turn left onto Rte 602. Drive 3 miles to the parking area, following the signs. The road eventually becomes Rte 707, then Rte 600. The park website has a page dedicated to preparing for this hike. Check it out before you head out.

Big Meadows HIKING
(Skyline Dr) A very popular area with four easy to medium-difficulty hikes. The Lewis Falls and Rose River trails run by the park's most spectacular waterfalls; the former accesses the Appalachian Trail.

Bearfence Mountain HIKING
(p23)

Skyland HIKING
(Skyline Dr) There are four easy trails here, none exceeding 1.6 miles, with a few steep sections throughout. The Stony Man Trail gives great views for not-too-strenuous trekking.

Traces Trail HIKING
One of the easiest and prettiest day hikes in the park, this 1.7-mile round-trip is a good bet for small children. The 'traces' you'll pass include an old mountain settlement, as the trail winds through a cool, mature oak forest. Start from the Mathews Arm Campground, where the trail quickly winds past pieces of former foundations and roads. Enveloped in a canopy of red oaks, the trail soon rises above the campground amphitheater. Near the end of the trail, a solitary oak stands like a beacon, and there are points ahead where you can take in mountain vistas.

Shenandoah National Park

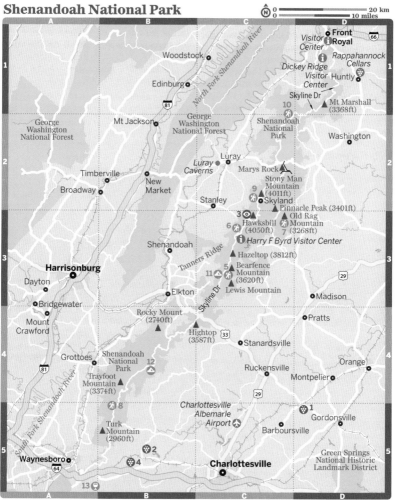

Shenandoah National Park

Skyland Stables HORSEBACK RIDING
(p21)

Riprap Trail HIKING
(Skyline Dr) Three trails of varying difficulty. Blackrock Summit is a moderately easy 1-mile loop that yields fantastic vistas from a viewpoint. It's suitable for kids. Then there is the moderate 3.4-mile trail to Chimney Rock (p50) and the fairly strenuous 9.8-mile Riprap Loop that connects with the Appalachian Trail.

🛏️ Sleeping

Big Meadows Campground CAMPGROUND $
(☑ 877-444-6777; www.recreation.gov; Mile 51.3, Skyline Dr; tent & RV sites $20; ☺ May-Oct) Find the perfect spot among 217 non-electric sites and you might just snap a quick photo of a resident bear lumbering past your campfire. This campground tends to be crowded, especially during fall, but it's smack in the middle of Skyline Drive, has good facilities (flush toilets, showers, store, laundry) and is a convenient base for all exploration.

Loft Mountain CAMPGROUND $
(☑ 434-823-4675; www.recreation.gov; Mile 79.5, Skyline Dr; tent & RV sites $15; ☺ May-Oct) This 'lofty' campground features some serious altitude and views on top of Big Flat Mountain. It's also the largest in the park, so expect crowds. Facilities include flush toilets, showers, laundry, drinking water, dump station and store selling firewood and provisions. There's no electricity to sites.

Mathews Arm CAMPGROUND $
(☑ 540-999-3132; www.recreation.gov; Mile 22.1, Skyline Dr; tent & RV sites $15; ☺ May-Oct) This is the first campground reached when entering from the north. It offers flush toilets, drinking water, a dump station and a hiking trail to a waterfall, but there's no store or electricity to sites.

Lewis Mountain CAMPGROUND $
(☑ 540-999-3500; www.recreation.gov; Mile 37.5, Skyline Dr; tent sites $15; ☺ Apr-Oct) One of the smaller, more secluded spots (available on a first-come, first-serve basis), with just 31 non-electric sites and a camp store.

Lewis Mountain Cabins CABIN $
(☑ 855-470-6005; www.goshenandoah.com; Mile 57.6, Skyline Dr; 1- & 2-bed cabins $133-138, d bunk cabins $37-42; ☺ early Mar-late Nov; 🅿️ 🐾) The most rustic accommodation option in the area short of camping, this place has several

pleasantly furnished one- and two-bedroom cabins complete with private bathrooms for a hot shower after a day's hiking. There are also small cabins with bunk beds, but no linen or bathroom. Bear in mind many cabins are attached, although we've never heard our neighbors here.

Skyland Resort RESORT $$
(☑ 855-470-6005; www.goshenandoah.com; Mile 41.7, Skyline Dr; r $141-265, cabins $130-281; ☺ late Mar–mid-Nov; 🅿️ ❄️ 📶 🐾) Founded in 1888, this spectacularly located resort commands views over the countryside. There's a variety of room types, including recently renovated premium rooms, rustic but comfy cabins, a taproom with a live entertainment program, and a full-service dining room. You can arrange horseback rides from here. Opens a month or so before Big Meadows in the spring.

Wi-fi access is in the main lodge only.

Big Meadows Lodge LODGE $$
(☑ 855-470-6005; www.goshenandoah.com; Mile 51.2, Skyline Dr; r $122-206, cabins $140-145; ☺ early May-early Nov; 🅿️ ❄️ 📶) Historic Big Meadows Lodge has 29 cozy wood-paneled rooms and five rustic cabins. The on-site Spottswood Dining Room serves three hearty meals a day; reserve well in advance. Free, family-friendly entertainment is presented nightly in the bar.

🍴 Eating

Pollock Dining Room AMERICAN $$
(www.visitshenandoah.com; Mile 41.7, Skyline Dr, Skyland Resort; lunch mains $9-20, dinner mains $12-28; ☺ 7:30-10:30am, noon-2:30pm & 5-9pm late Mar-late Nov) The food is solid, if not life altering, in Skyland's dining room. But the view of the leafy park though the big windows? Now that's a different story. Lunch means sandwiches and burgers, while dinner aims a little fancier – stick to classics like Rapidan Camp Trout and Roosevelt Chicken. The adjacent taproom (2pm to 10pm) serves cocktails, local beers and a limited menu of sandwiches and a few specialties.

Spottswood Dining Room AMERICAN $$
(www.visitshenandoah.com; Mile 51.3, Skyline Dr, Big Meadows Lodge; lunch mains $8-17, dinner mains $12-28; ☺ 7:30-10am, noon-2pm & 5:30-9pm early May-early Nov; ☑) The wide-ranging menu at the dining room in Big Meadows Lodge makes the most of locally sourced ingredients. Complement your food with Virginian wines and local microbrews, all enjoyed in

an old-fashioned rustic-lodge ambience. There's also a taproom (2pm to 11pm) with a limited menu and live entertainment. It's also possible to source boxed lunches here.

ℹ️ Information

There are two visitor centers in the park. Both have maps and backcountry permits, as well as information about outdoor activities.

Dickey Ridge (www.nps.gov/shen; Mile 4.6, Skyline Dr; ⊙ 9am-5pm Mon-Fri, to 6pm Sat & Sun, closed late Nov-early Apr) In the north.

Harry F Byrd (www.nps.gov/shen; Mile 51, Skyline Dr; ⊙ 9am-5pm late Mar-late Nov, 9:30am-4pm Fri-Sun late Nov-late Mar) In the south.

ℹ️ Getting There & Away

You'll really need your own wheels to explore the length and breadth of the park, which can be easily accessed from several exits off I-81. The **Virginia Breeze** (📞 877-462-6342; www.catch thevabreeze.com; tickets $15-50) bus service to/from Washington, DC, stops at Front Royal and Staunton near the main park entrances/exits. Amtrak (p65) runs train services between DC and Staunton.

There is a **gas station** (📞 540-999-2211; Mile 51.2, Skyline Dr; ⊙ 8am-8pm) at Big Meadows Wayside.

Staunton

📞 540 / POP 24,363

This small-town beauty has much going for it, including a historic and walkable town center, a fantastic foodie scene, great microbreweries, regular live music downtown and a first-rate theater. Add to this an abundance of outdoor activities nearby and you may find yourself looking into local real estate when you get here.

◉ Sights

The pedestrian-friendly, handsome town center boasts more than 200 buildings designed by noted Victorian architect TJ Collins. There's an artsy yet unpretentious bohemian vibe thanks to the presence of Mary Baldwin, a small liberal arts university.

Ox-Eye Vineyard Tasting Room   WINERY
(📞 540-849-7926; www.oxeyevineyards.com; 44 Middlebrook Ave; tasting $7; ⊙ noon-6pm Mon-Thu, to 7pm Fri, 10am-7pm Sat, noon-5pm Sun) Ox-Eye is known for its cool-climate reds and whites (particularly its dry rieslings, Lemberger

and pinot noir). Its wharf district tasting room occupies a handsome building dating from 1904 and is a pleasant stop when wandering through town. Light fare ($5.50 to $8) is available to enjoy with your tasting.

Frontier Culture Museum   MUSEUM
(📞 540-332-7850; www.frontiermuseum.org; 1290 Richmond Rd; adult/student/child 6-12yr $12/11/7; ⊙ 9am-5pm mid-Mar-Nov, 10am-4pm Dec-mid-Mar) The excellent Frontier Culture Museum is cooler than its name might suggest. On the 100-plus acre grounds you'll find authentic historic buildings from Germany, Ireland and England, plus re-created West African dwellings and a separate area of American frontier dwellings. Costumed interpreters (aided by bleating livestock) do an excellent job showing what life was like for the disparate ancestors of today's Virginians.

Woodrow Wilson Presidential Library   HISTORIC SITE
(p27)

🛏️ Sleeping

Storefront   APARTMENT $$
(📞 804-218-5656; www.the-storefront-hotel.com; 14 S New St; r Sun-Thu $115, Fri-Sun $159) It dubs itself a very small hotel, but this hip getaway is really a narrow building with one two-story apartment. The front door opens onto a sitting area and bar. Upstairs you'll find a kitchen and bedroom. Two-night minimum stay Friday and Saturday.

Frederick House   B&B $$
(📞 540-885-4220; www.frederickhouse.com; 28 N New St; r $135-155, ste $170-230; 🅿 ❄ 🛜 🛁 🐾) Genial owners Ross and Brooke Williams work hard to ensure that guests at their downtown guesthouse are happy. Rooms are scattered throughout five historical residences with 23 varied rooms and suites – all with private bathrooms and some with air-con. The nicest rooms are in Patrick House (request room 26). Breakfast is included in the price.

Stonewall Jackson Hotel   HOTEL $$
(📞 540-885-4848; www.stonewalljacksonhotel.com; 24 S Market St; r $119-250; 🅿 ❄ 🛜 🛁 🐾) Once a showcase of the restrained Southern style of the classical commonwealth, Staunton's best-known hotel is looking dowdy these days and is in sore need of a full makeover. That said, rooms are comfortable enough, rates are reasonable and there's an on-site gym, indoor pool and bar.

Staunton

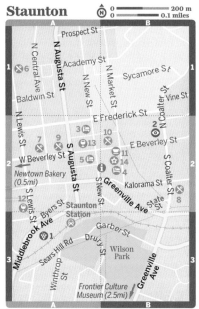

0 ——— 200 m
0 ——— 0.1 miles

✖ Eating

The dining scene is remarkably strong for a such a small city and offers choices to please almost every palate and budget. It's best to reserve your table in advance, especially on nights when there is a show at the Blackfriars Playhouse.

A bustling spring-to-autumn **farmers market** (www.stauntonfarmersmarket.org) is held on Saturdays in the carpark near the train station.

Split Banana Co.   ICE CREAM
(☑ 866-492-3668; www.thesplitbanana.com; 7 W Beverley St; one scoop $2.70; ⊙ noon-11pm; ♿) This locals' favorite ice cream parlor has delicious flavors, served up in a charmingly old-fashioned setting. Open late.

★ Chicano Boy   MEXICAN $
(☑ 540-569-2105; www.chicanoboytaco.com; 240 N Central Ave, suite 6; tacos $9, burritos $10; ⊙ 11am-2pm & 5-9pm Tue-Sat; ♿♿) This taquería's $7 lunch deal is great value, with a drink, a dip and two tacos. Prices don't rise much at dinner, when tacos – including the Al Pastor (pork marinated in chilli and pineapple), vegetarian (sweet potato and black bean) and vegan (soy protein, tomato, olives, capers) – run out the door. Eat in or take out.

Newtown Bakery   BAKERY, PIZZERIA $
(☑ 540-885-3799; www.newtownbaking.com; 960 W Beverley St; sandwiches $6-9, pizzas $10-14; ⊙ 7:30am-3pm & 5-9pm Wed-Fri, 8am-2pm & 5-9pm Sat; P♿♿) This is the type of place that every small town needs. It bakes its own European-style bread and pastries, serves soup and sandwiches at lunch, and cranks up the wood-fired pizza oven at night to offer piping hot, super-tasty pies. Coffee is from the Staunton Coffee Company, and wine and beer are available too. Love it.

Farmhouse Kitchen & Wares   CAFE $
(☑ 540-712-7791; www.farmhousekitchenandwares. com; 101 W Beverly St; breakfast dishes $6-11, sandwiches $9-12.50; ⊙ 8am-3pm Mon-Sat) The delicious gourmet sandwiches are piled high at this country-chic cafe, where you can also purchase any of the stylish cookware on display. Homemade breakfasts too.

★ Shack   AMERICAN $$
(☑ 540-490-1961; www.theshackva.com; 105 S Coalter St; brunch mains $12-22, dinner 3-/4-course prix-fixe $45/55; ⊙ 5-9pm Wed-Sat, 10:30am-2pm Sun; ♿) It may be cooked and served in a small and unadorned space (hence the name), but the dishes served here are among the best in the state. Chef Ian Boden, a two-time James Beard semi-finalist, makes the most of seasonal local produce in his menu, which is inspired by his mountain roots and

Eastern European Jewish heritage. Good wine list.

Zynodoa SOUTHERN US $$$
(☑540-885-7775; www.zynodoa.com; 115 E Beverley St; mains $21-34; ☺5-9:30pm Sun-Tue, to 10:30pm Wed-Sat; ☑) Local farms and wineries are the backbone of Zynodoa's larder, and the chef delivers his predominantly Southern dishes (vegetable succotash, cornmeal-crusted wild blue catfish, apple cider–braised pork, Rappahannock River fried oysters) in a sleekly designed dining room. Its location makes it a favoured destination for pre-theater dinners.

☕ Drinking & Entertainment

Yelping Dog WINE BAR
(☑540-885-2275; www.yelpingdogwine.com; 9 E Beverly St; ☺11am-9pm Tue-Thu, to 10pm Fri & Sat, noon-6pm Sun) An inviting wine bar in the thick of the downtown action, the Yelping Dog has its priorities right: wine, cheese and charcuterie. It also serves craft beer. If you're on the fence about ordering one of the gourmet grilled cheese sandwiches ($9 to $10), go ahead and fall off. They're delicious. Live music some Saturday nights.

Redbeard Brewery MICROBREWERY
(www.redbeardbrews.com; 102 S Lewis St; ☺noon-11pm Tue-Sun) A small-batch brewery that serves up tasty IPAs, saisons, ambers and other seasonal selections. Live music every Friday from 9pm, and an open jam session on Tuesdays from 7:30pm. Food trucks usually congregate here from Thursday to Sunday.

By & By CAFE
(☑540-887-0041; 140 E Beverley St; bagels $1.50-5.50, sandwiches $6.50-8; ☺7:30am-6pm Mon-Thu, to 7pm Fri & Sat, 10am-3pm Sun; ☂) Serving Staunton's best coffee (espresso, drip, French press), as well as pastries and bagels from Newtown Bakery (p70), this cafe is inevitably filled with locals catching up with friends or settling into a couch or armchair to take advantage of the free wi-fi and indulge in a bit of telecommuting.

★ **Blackfriars Playhouse** THEATER
(☑540-851-1733; www.americanshakespearecenter. com; 10 S Market St; tickets $29-49) Don't leave Staunton without catching a show at the Blackfriars Playhouse, where actors from the American Shakespeare Center perform in a re-creation of Shakespeare's original indoor theater. The acting is up-close and engaged, and brave guests can grab a seat on the side of the stage.

ℹ Information

Visitor Center (☑540-332-3971; www.visit staunton.com; 35 S New St; ☺9am-6pm Apr-Oct, 9:30am-5:30pm Nov-Mar) Helpful office for tourism advice and brochures.

ℹ Getting There & Away

Staunton sits beside I-81, not far from the junction with I-64 E. **Amtrak** (www.amtrak.com; 1 Middlebrook Ave) trains stop here three times per week on their way to/from Charlottesville and Washington, DC.

Lexington
☑540 / POP 7045
The fighting spirit of the South is visually encapsulated by the sight of cadets from the Virginia Military Institute (VMI) strutting their stuff at Friday's full dress parade. The institute is one of Lexington's two major historic institutions, the other being Washington & Lee University (W&L). Two Civil War generals, Robert E Lee and Stonewall Jackson, lived here and are buried in town, and Lexington has long been a favorite stop for Civil War enthusiasts. Today you're as likely to see hikers, cyclists and paddlers using Lexington as a launchpad for adventures in the nearby Blue Ridge Mountains, where the Blue Ridge Parkway and the Appalachian Trail overlook the valley, as well as on the James River. The opening of new hotels, bars and restaurants has re-energized the city in recent years – it's a great Shenandoah base.

APPALACHIAN TRAIL
The country's longest footpath stretches more than 2100 miles, crosses six national parks and slices through 14 states from Georgia to Maine. Deep woods, alpine peaks, cow-dotted farms and foraging bears are part of the landscape. An estimated two to three million people annually trek a portion of the Appalachian Trail, inhaling the fresh air and admiring the spectacular scenery. You'll find 544 miles of the trail crossing the western mountains of Virginia, also home to the oft-photographed McAfee Knob (p29) near Roanoke.

◉ Sights & Activities

Civil War sites and historic buildings cluster downtown and on the nearby campuses of Washington & Lee and the Virginia Military Institute, which sit side-by-side. All of these sites are within an easy stroll of each other. The visitor center (p74) can supply an informative walking tour map.

Washington & Lee University   UNIVERSITY
(☏540-458-8400; www.wlu.edu) Named for George Washington and Robert E Lee, this pretty and preppy liberal arts college was founded in 1749. George Washington saved the young school in 1796 with a gift of $20,000. Confederate general Robert E Lee served as president after the Civil War in the hope of unifying the country through education. Visitors today can stroll along the striking red-brick Colonnade and visit **Lee Chapel & Museum** (☏540-458-8768; www.wlu.edu/lee-chapel-and-museum; adult/child $5/3; ⊙9am-4pm Mon-Sat, 1-4pm Sun Nov-Mar, to 5pm Apr-Oct).

Note that doors on the garage stall of the university president's house will likely be open. While president of the school, Lee left the door ajar for his wandering horse Traveller. Today, tradition keeps them open in case Traveller's ghost wanders home.

Stonewall Jackson House   HISTORIC BUILDING
(☏540-464-7704; www.stonewalljackson.org; 8 E Washington St; adult/child 6-17yr $8/6; ⊙9am-5pm Mon-Sat, from 1pm Sun) One of the most revered generals of the south, Thomas Jonathon 'Stonewall' Jackson lived in this handsome brick Federal-style town house with his wife and five slaves from 1851 to 1861, while he taught at nearby VMI. The house is remarkably well preserved, and 45-minute guided tours provide fascinating insight into Jackson's life and times. His body (all but his left arm, anyway) is buried in the cemetery a few blocks away.

Virginia Military Institute   UNIVERSITY
(VMI; www.vmi.edu; Letcher Ave) You'll either be impressed or put off by the extreme discipline of the cadets at Virginia Military Institute, the only university to have sent its entire graduating class into combat (plaques to student war dead are touching and ubiquitous). The **VMI Museum** (☏540-464-7334; www.vmi.edu/museum; 415 Letcher Ave; $5; ⊙9am-5pm) houses the stuffed carcass of Stonewall Jackson's horse among its 15,000 artifacts and the **George C Marshall Museum** (☏540-463-2083; www.marshallfoundation.org/museum; VMI Parade; adult/student/child under 13yr $5/2/free; ⊙11am-4pm Tue-Sat) honors the creator of the Marshall Plan for post-WWII European reconstruction.

Contact the museum for a free 45-minute cadet-guided tour of the campus, offered at noon during term time. A full-dress parade takes place most Fridays at 4pm during the school year.

Upper James River Water Trail   CANOEING
(www.upperjamesriverwatertrail.com; Botetourt) This new 74-mile paddling trail follows the James River as it flows through the foothills of the Blue Ridge Mountains toward Richmond and the coast. The trail is divided into various sections taking between one and seven hours to traverse by canoe or kayak.

Twin River Outfitters   CANOEING; TUBING
(☏540-254-8012; https://canoevirginia.net; 640 Lowe St, Buchanan; paddling trips from $34; ⊙9am-5pm Apr-Oct) Scan for eagles and deer as you paddle or tube down the James River on the new Upper James River Paddling Trail with this popular outfitter, owned by twin brothers. Mileage and travel times vary, as does difficulty. A shuttle ride is included in the price.

🛏 Sleeping

B&Bs and a boutique hotel can be found on Main St downtown. Chain hotels abound beside the junction of I-81 and I-64. The top accommodations fill up on weekends in fall and spring when there are events at the colleges, but you can usually snag a room at one of the chains by using a third-party booking service.

Grace House   B&B $$
(☏571-286-8411; www.gracehouselexva.com; 506 S Main St; r from $140; 🅿🛜) There are plenty of upmarket B&Bs in Virginia, but few are as stylish as this one. In an 1890 building that once functioned as Grace Presbyterian Church, it offers four elegant guest rooms with attached or adjoining private bathrooms. There's also a comfortable guest lounge.

★ Georges   BOUTIQUE HOTEL $$$
(☏540-463-2500; www.thegeorges.com; 11 N Main St; r $170-310, ste $310-460; 🅿❄🛜) Set in two historic buildings on opposite sides of Main St, Georges has 18 classy rooms featuring high-end furnishings and luxury linens. The great location, friendly service and delicious breakfast (included in the room rate) make

Lexington

Lexington

it Lexington's best accommodation option, and put it in the running for the accolade of best in the Shenandoah too.

✕ Eating

Pure Eats AMERICAN $
(⌨540-462-6000; www.pure-eats.com; 107 N Main St; burgers $7-12, doughnuts $1.25; ⊙8am-8pm) In a former filling station, Pure Eats doles out delicious house-made doughnuts and egg-and-cheese biscuits in the morning; later in the day, burgers are the popular choice. Also sells local craft brews, milkshakes made with local milk and ice cream from a local creamery.

Blue Sky Bakery SANDWICHES $
(⌨540-463-6546; 125 W Nelson St; soup $4, sandwiches $8; ⊙10:30am-4pm Mon-Fri) This local favorite has tasty focaccia sandwiches, hearty soups and fresh salads. Unfortunately, it is closed on weekends.

★ Red Hen FRENCH $$$
(⌨540-464-4401; www.redhenlex.com; 11 E Washington St; mains $22-28; ⊙5-9:30pm Tue-Sat; ⌖) 🍃 Reserve well ahead for a memorable meal at Red Hen, an intimate restaurant occupying an 1890 building just off Main St. The limited menu features a creative, French-focused menu showcasing fine local produce. Great cocktails too.

Southern Inn AMERICAN $$$
(⌨540-463-3612; www.southerninn.com; 37 S Main St; mains $16-35; ⊙11:30am-10pm Mon-Sat, 10am-9pm Sun) There's an old-fashioned feel at this popular eatery on Lexington's main

KRISTI BLOKHIN / SHUTTERSTOCK ©

Washington & Lee University (p72), Lexington

drag. The food could be better (though our most-recent meal featured excellent produce, dishes were poorly executed), but the surrounds and staff are welcoming.

Drinking & Entertainment

Taps BAR
(☏ 540-463-2500; www.thegeorges.com; 11 Main St; ⊗ 3-10pm Mon-Thu, 11am-11pm Fri & Sat) This cozy place in Georges hotel doubles as Lexington's living room, with students, professors and other locals hanging out on the fancy couches or at the small bar. Come here for craft beer, fine cocktails and local gossip. There's also a short pub-grub menu (sandwiches $9 to $11).

Pronto COFFEE
(☏ 540-464-1472; www.prontogelateria.com; 26 S Main St; ⊗ 8am-8pm Wed-Mon) Serves the best espresso coffee in town. Also worth a stop for its creamy gelatos (one scoop $2.70) and grab-and-go gourmet sandwiches ($6 to $7.50).

Hull's Drive-in CINEMA
(☏ 540-463-2621; www.hullsdrivein.com; 2367 N Lee Hwy/US 11; adult/child 5-11yr $7/3; ⊗ gates open 6:30pm Fri & Sat Mar-Oct; ⊞) For old-fashioned amusement, catch a movie at this 1950s drive-in movie theater, set 5.5 miles north of Lexington. Movies start 20 minutes after sunset. Concession stand sells burgers, popcorn, sno-cones.

🔒 Shopping

There's an arts and crafts precinct known as 'Gallery Row' on Washington St where shops and galleries sell works by local artisans and artists.

ℹ Information

Visitor Center (☏ 540-463-3777; www. LexingtonVirginia.com; 106 E Washington St; ⊗ 8am-6pm Jun-Aug, 8:30am-5:30pm Sep & Oct, 9am-5pm Nov-May) In a central downtown location, the visitor center has loads of info on Lexington and the surrounding area. It also has a good walking tour map of historic buildings downtown. The website is a great resource for nearby outdoor adventures.

ℹ Getting There & Away

Lexington sits at the junction of I-81 and I-64. The closest airport is Roanoke-Blacksburg Regional Airport (p77), which is 55 miles south. The Virginia Breeze (p69) bus service from DC travels here daily via Front Royal, Harrisonburg and Staunton and continues to Christianburg and Blacksburg before returning along the same route.

ℹ Getting Around

Street parking is free, but is limited to two hours. The carpark at the visitor center is free and without time limits.

BLUE RIDGE HIGHLANDS & SOUTHWEST VIRGINIA

The Blue Ridge Highlands and the Roanoke Valley are two of the most attractive regions in the state, with farm-dotted valleys unfurling between the Blue Ridge and Allegheny Mountains. The Blue Ridge Parkway and Appalachian Trail roll across the mountains here, which are home to scenic rivers, streams and lakes. Old-time mountain music can be heard regularly, and wineries and craft breweries offer tastings in small towns and on mountain slopes. The most rugged part of the region – and the state – is the southwestern tip of Virginia, where mountain music was born. Turn onto any side road and you'll plunge into dark strands of dogwood and fir, and see fast streams and white waterfalls. You might even hear banjos twanging and feet stomping in the distance.

❶ Information

Bedford Area Welcome Center (Visit Bedford; 540-587-5681; www.visitbedford.com; 816 Burks Hill Rd, Bedford; ⊙ 9am-5pm; 🛜) Stop at this office to buy tickets for the D-Day memorial and to source information about regional attractions. Offers public restrooms and wi-fi.

Mount Rogers Park Headquarters (276-783-5196, 800-628-7202; www.fs.usda.gov; 3714 Hwy 16, Marion; ⊙ 8am-4:30pm Mon-Fri) This center can provide maps and recreation directories.

❶ Getting There & Away

To explore the byways and country roads, you will need a car. The primary interstate here is I-81, running north–south through the western edge of the state. The Blue Ridge Parkway runs parallel to I-81, but it is much slower going.

Roanoke is served by Amtrak, with daily services linking it to New York (tickets from $75, 9½ hours) and Washington, DC (tickets from $37, five hours). The major airport in the region is the Roanoke-Blacksburg Regional Airport (p77).

Roanoke

540 / POP 98,660

Illuminated by the giant star atop Mill Mountain, Roanoke is the largest city in the Roanoke Valley and is the self-proclaimed 'Capital of the Blue Ridge.' Close to the Blue Ridge Parkway and the Appalachian Trail, it's a convenient base camp for exploring the great outdoors. An expanding greenway

system, a burgeoning arts scene and a slowly growing portfolio of farm-to-table restaurants have energized the city in recent years, flipping Roanoke from sleepy to almost hip.

◉ Sights

★ **O. Winston Link Museum**   MUSEUM
(540-982-5465; http://roanokehistory.org; 101 Shenandoah Ave NE; adult/child 3-11yr $6/5; ⊙ 10am-5pm Tue-Sat) Trainspotters aren't the only ones who will find this museum fascinating. It is home to a large collection of photographs, sound recordings and film by O Winston Link (1914–2001), a New Yorker who in the 1950s spent nine months recording the last years of steam power on the Norfolk and Western Railway. The gelatin silver prints of Link's black-and-white photographs are hugely atmospheric – many were shot at night, a rarity at the time – and are very dramatic.

Taubman Museum of Art   MUSEUM
(540-342-5760; www.taubmanmuseum.org; 110 Salem Ave SE; ⊙ 10am-5pm Wed-Sat, noon-5pm Sun, to 9pm 3rd Thu & 1st Fri of month; P) FREE
The jewel in Roanoke's cultural crown, this impressive museum is set in a sculptural steel-and-glass edifice. Inside, you'll find a small permanent collection strong in 19th- and 20th-century American works including Norman Rockwell's crowd-pleasing *Framed* (1946) and Winslow Homer's *Woodchopper in the Adirondacks* (c 1870). Four temporary exhibition galleries host everything from craft to video to installation art.

Center in the Square   MUSEUM
(540-342-5700; www.centerinthesquare.org; 1 Market Sq; ⊙ 10am-5pm Tue-Sat, from 1pm Sun) The city's cultural heartbeat, where you'll find three museums, a butterfly garden, aquariums and a theater. The museums cover

---

BLUE RIDGE PARKWAY: VIRGINIA CAMPGROUNDS

Rocky Knob Campground (877-444-6777; www.recreation.gov; Mile 167.1, Blue Ridge Pkwy; tent & RV sites $20; ⊙ May-late Oct)

Otter Creek Campground (434-299-5125; www.recreation.gov; Mile 60.8, Blue Ridge Pkwy; tent & RV sites $20; ⊙ May-Oct; P)

Peaks of Otter Campground (p28)

DIRTY DANCING: MOUNTAIN LAKE HOTEL

On the shore of Mountain Lake, **Mountain Lake Hotel** (☑540-626-7172; www.mountainlakehotel.com; 115 Hotel Circle, Pembroke; r $170-228, ste & cottage $332) is a stalwart of Appalachian tourism. It doubled as the Catskills resort 'Kellerman's' in a little old movie called *Dirty Dancing*; four theme weekends offer dance lessons and film-related fun. On-site dining and drinking options range from a restaurant to a tavern and cafe. Activities include hiking, bocce, tennis, an outdoor pool and a treetop adventure course.

African American culture, pinball and science. The atrium aquariums and green rooftop can be visited free of charge; admission fees apply for other attractions.

Roanoke Star & Mill Mountain Park   PARK

(☑540-853-2236; www.playroanoke.com; 2000 JP Fishburn Pkwy) Mill Mountain Park has walking trails, a discovery center, a zoo (adult $9, child aged three to 11 years $7) and grand views of Roanoke. It's also home to the massive **Roanoke Star**, which shines over the city at night. You can drive up (via Walnut Ave SE) or hike up (take the Monument Trail just off Sylvan Ave SE or the Star Trail near Riverland Rd SE).

🛏 Sleeping

Rose Hill   B&B $

(☑540-400-7785; www.bandbrosehill.com; 521 Washington Ave SW; r $100-125; P🐾) This welcoming and traditional three-room B&B in Roanoke's historic district overlooks Highland Park close to downtown. Two rooms have external private bathrooms, the third has an en suite bathroom. Guests must be aged over 10.

Hotel Roanoke   HOTEL $$$

(☑540-985-5900; www.hotelroanoke.com; 110 Shenandoah Ave NW; r from $129; P@🐾🍽) This Tudor-style grand dame has presided over this city at the base of the Blue Ridge Mountains for more than a century. Now part of the Hilton Group, it's in desperate need of refurbishment. Rooms are adequate

only; service can be lackadaisical. A covered elevated walkway links the hotel with the downtown precinct.

🍴 Eating

Texas Tavern   DINER $

(☑540-342-4825; www.texastavern-inc.com; 114 W Church Ave; burgers $1.50-2.75, chile $1.90; ⊙24hr) Wait. What? A hamburger or hot dog for only $1.50? Yep, the food is cheap and tasty at the legendary Texas Tavern, a boxcar-sized diner that opened in 1930. The infamous cheesy western is a burger topped with a fried egg, cheese, relish, pickles and onions. Get one.

⭐ **Lucky**   MODERN AMERICAN $$

(☑540-982-1249; www.eatatlucky.com; 18 Kirk Ave SW; mains $18-30; ⊙5-9pm Mon-Wed, to 10pm Thu-Sat) Lucky has excellent cocktails (try 'The Cube') and a seasonally inspired menu of small plates (hickory-smoked porchetta, roasted oysters) and heartier mains (buttermilk fried chicken, morel and asparagus gnocchi). It also operates the equally wonderful Italian restaurant **Fortunato** (www.fortunatoroanoke.com) a few doors down, where the wood-fired pizzas are the stuff of dreams and poems.

Local Roots   MODERN AMERICAN $$

(☑540-206-2610; www.localrootsrestaurant.com; 1314 Grandin Rd SW; lunch mains $10-16, dinner mains $26-34; ⊙11am-2pm & 5-10pm Tue-Sat, 10:30am-2:30pm & 5-9pm Sun) Located in a shopping strip 2.6 miles west of the town center, this welcoming farm-to-table restaurant serves up tasty organic dishes. A large portion of the menu rotates seasonally. It's a good place to try bison, rainbow trout and other local produce. At lunch, sandwiches (including an excellent burger) dominate the menu.

WildFlour Restaurant & Bakery   INTERNATIONAL $$

(☑540-343-4543; http://wildflour4thst.com; 1212 4th St SW; sandwiches under $10, dinner mains $16-24; ⊙11am-9pm Mon-Sat; P) Give us our daily bread. We mean that – give us your daily Wildlflour bread selection, especially French cornmeal on Mondays. Then there are the wonderful homemade sandwiches and rustic fusion-meets-New-American menu, with entrees including a hearty-as-hell meatloaf with a mound of mashed potato.

🍷 Drinking

Microbreweries have been popping up across town and there's a popular bar at Hotel Roanoke.

Ballast Point   BREWERY
(☑ 540-591-3059; www.ballastpoint.com; 555 International Pkwy, Daleville; ⊘ 11am-9pm Mon-Thu, to 11pm Fri & Sat, 10am-9pm Sun) You'll find bold brews and rugged views at this new outpost of the famed San Diego brewery. Folks from miles around gather on the patio to sip one of the 35 beers on tap, with local mountains as the backdrop. The brewery, which also serves gourmet pub fare, is 18 miles north of downtown Roanoke off I-81.

🛍 Shopping

⭐ **Black Dog Salvage**   ANTIQUES
(☑ 540-343-6200; www.blackdogsalvage.com; 902 13th St SW; ⊘ 9am-5pm Mon-Sat, from noon Sun) As seen on the cable show *Salvage Dogs*, the folks at this sprawling antique shop sell doors and doorknobs, light fixtures, wrought iron, and vintage plumbing and hardware. Basically, it's filled with architecturally unique old house parts and fixtures that have been reclaimed and re-purposed, plus random antiques. Stop by, it's a welcoming place filled with unexpected treasures.

ℹ Information

Blue Ridge Visitor Information Center
(☑ 540-342-6025; www.visitroanokeva.com; 101 Shenandoah Ave NE; ⊘ 9am-5pm daily Mar-Dec, 9am-5pm Mon-Sat, noon-5pm Sun Jan & Feb; 🛜) Helpful office supplying information about Roanoke and Virginia's Blue Ridge region.

ℹ Getting There & Away

Amtrak operates daily services between Roanoke and New York (tickets from $75, 9½ hours) on the Northeast Regional line. These leave from the downtown **train station** (www.amtrak.com; 55 Norfolk Avenue SW) and travel via Washington, DC (tickets from $37, five hours).

Roanoke-Blacksburg Regional Airport
(☑ 540-362-1999; www.roanokeairport.com; 5202 Aviation Dr NW) is 5 miles north of downtown and serves the Roanoke and Shenandoah Valley regions. If you're driving, I-81 and I-581 link to the city. The Blue Ridge Parkway is just 5 miles from downtown.

Floyd

🎵 540 / POP 440

Tucked in the foothills of the Blue Ridge Mountains close to the Blue Ridge Parkway, tiny, cute-as-a-postcard Floyd isn't much more than an intersection between Hwy 8 and Hwy 221. In fact, the whole county only has one stoplight. But life explodes on Friday nights during the Friday Night Jamboree at the Floyd Country Store and the surrounding sidewalks when folks from far and wide converge for a night of live old-time music and communal good cheer.

🎉 Festivals & Events

Floydfest   MUSIC
(www.floydfest.com; 894 Rock Castle Gorge Rd; ⊘ late July) Southern rock, modern bluegrass, folk music and jam bands, it's all here on eight stages for five days, just off the Blue Ridge Parkway. Past performers include Shakey Graves, Trampled by Turtles, Shovels and Rope, and Brandy Carlyle.

🛏 Sleeping & Eating

⭐ **Hotel Floyd**   HOTEL $
(☑ 540-745-6080; www.hotelfloyd.com; 300 Rick Lewis Way; r $99-140, ste $150-180; P ❄ @ 🛜 🐾) There may not be much style on show at this place, but who cares? Rooms are large, impeccably clean and very comfortable. Service is friendly, breakfast is included in the room rate and Main St is only a short walk away. It's cheap, too. All of this makes it deservedly popular, so book ahead.

Dogtown Roadhouse   PIZZA $
(☑ 540-745-6836; www.dogtownroadhouse.com; 302 S Locust St; pizzas $10-18; ⊘ 4-9pm Wed & Thu, 4pm-midnight Fri, noon-midnight Sat, noon-9pm Sun) You might see a local farmer walk in with produce for the toppings at this lively pizzeria, which serves wood-fired pies including the Appalachian (apple butter base, sausage, caramelized onion, cheddar and goat cheeses). Lagers, stouts, porters and ciders are on tap, and there's live rock on Friday and Saturday nights from 8pm.

Pine Tavern   AMERICAN $
(☑ 540-745-4482; www.thepinetavern.com; 611 Floyd Hwy N; mains $10-17; ⊘ 4:30-9pm Fri, from noon Sat, 11am-8pm Sun; P ♿) One taste of the buttermilk biscuits, fried chicken and country ham at this all-you-can-eat family-style restaurant and your mouth won't stop

salivating. We thoroughly approve of the way they pile on dumplings, pinto beans, green beans and mashed potatoes. There's occasional live music in the outside pavilion during spring and summer.

Drinking & Entertainment

★ Chateau Morrisette
WINERY

(☎ 540-593-2865; www.thedogs.com; 287 Winery Rd, Mile 171.5 off Blue Ridge Pkwy; tastings incl glass $10; ⊙ 10am-5pm Mon-Thu, to 6pm Fri & Sat, 11am-5pm Sun) The Blue Ridge Mountains form an attractive backdrop at this winery 13 miles southwest of Floyd. Head to the swish tasting room to try the signature Black Dog dry red or the Our Dog Blue, a blend of riesling, Traminette and Vidal Blanc. There's also a restaurant (open 11am to 2pm Wednesday and Thursday, to 8pm Friday and Saturday, and to 3pm Sunday) serving a cheese and charcuterie plate ($19) and burgers ($13 to $15) at lunch and more upmarket fare at dinner (mains $28 to $40).

★ Floyd Country Store
LIVE MUSIC

(☎ 540-745-4563; www.floydcountrystore.com; 206 S Locust St; ⊙ 10am-5pm Mon-Thu, to 10:30pm Fri, to 6pm Sat, 11am-6pm Sun) This place is why most folk come to Floyd, especially for the Friday Night Jamboree, which starts at 6:30pm. For $5, you get three bluegrass bands in four hours and the chance to watch happy crowds jam to regional heritage music. No smokin', no drinkin', but there's plenty of dancin' (of the flat footing style) and good cheer.

There are also performances on weekend days; on warm nights you'll likely catch music jams on the sidewalk outside. Every first Saturday of the month between May and September, the store hosts the live Floyd Radio Show from 7:30pm. Tickets cost $12 ($15 purchased on the night) and should be booked in advance.

❶ Getting There & Away

Floyd is 20 miles southeast of I-81 and is best reached by car. The closest major airport is Roanoke-Blacksburg Regional Airport (p77), about 50 miles north.

Galax
☑ 276 / POP 6780

Galax claims to be the world capital of mountain music, although it feels like anywhere-else-ville outside of the immedi-

ate downtown area, which is on the National Register of Historic Places. The town is an important stop on the 250-mile-long Crooked Road music trail, and is close to the Blue Ridge Parkway.

Festivals & Events

Old Fiddlers' Convention
MUSIC

(p39)

Sleeping & Eating

Doctor's Inn
INN $

(☎ 276-238-9998; www.thedoctorsinnvirginia.com; 406 W Stuart Dr; r $134; ⓟ❋🐾) A well-maintained and welcoming B&B in a heritage-listed 1903 house a few blocks from downtown Galax. Only one of the six rooms has its own bathroom. Excellent breakfasts included.

Fiddlers Roost
CABIN $$

(☎ 276-236-1212; www.fiddlersroostcabins.com; 485 Fishers Peak Rd; cabins $120-300; ⓟ) These eight cabins resemble Lincoln Logs playsets. The interiors are decorated in 'quilt' chic; they may not win a place in *Wallpaper* magazine, but they're cozy and have gas fireplaces, kitchens, TVs and DVD players. Breakfast included with all but Cabin on the Blue. Two-night minimum on weekends.

Galax Smokehouse
BARBECUE $

(☎ 276-236-1000; www.thegalaxsmokehouse.com; 101 N Main St; sandwiches $2-9, ribs $14-21; ⊙ 11am-9pm Mon-Sat, to 3pm Sun; 🐾) The pit BBQ at this local institution produces mighty fine, sweetly sauced Memphis-style meat.

Drinking & Entertainment

Creek Bottom Brews
MICROBREWERY

(☎ 276-236-2337; www.cbbrews.com; 307 N Meadow St; mains $6-16; ⊙ 11am-9pm Tue-Thu, to 10pm Fri & Sat) Has a changing line-up of its own craft brews, which go nicely with the brick-oven pizza and smoked chicken wings fired up on site. Try the Hellgrammite Brown Ale. The brewery is hidden behind a corrugated iron fence next to Pronets.

Blue Ridge Music Center
LIVE MUSIC

(p39)

Rex Theater
LIVE MUSIC

(p39)

Mount Rogers National Recreation Area

🛍 Shopping

Barr's Fiddle Shop MUSIC
(📞 276-236-2411; www.barrsfiddleshop.com; 105
S Main St; ⏰ 9am-5pm Mon-Sat) Tom Barr is
the Stradivarius of the mountains, a master
craftsman sought out by fiddle and mando-
lin aficionados across the world.

ℹ Getting There & Away

The best way to get to Galax is by car. The town
borders US 58 about 10 miles southwest of I-77.
Roanoke-Blacksburg Regional Airport (p77) is
90 miles northeast via I-77 north and I-81 N.
The city is about 10 miles from the Blue Ridge
Parkway.

Abingdon

📞 276 / POP 8080
One of the most photogenic towns in Virginia, Abingdon retains fine Federal and Victorian architecture in its historic district. The
long-running regional theater in the center
of town is a state-wide draw, as is the magnificent Virginia Creeper Trail. Popular with
cyclists and hikers, this leafy path down
from the mountains unfurls along an old
railroad bed.

👁 Sights & Activities

Mount Rogers
National Recreation Area NATURE RESERVE
(www.fs.usda.gov/gwj; Hwy 16, Marion) This seriously beautiful area is well worth a visit for outdoor enthusiasts. Hike, fish or
cross-country ski among ancient hardwood
trees and the state's tallest peak. The 33.4-
mile Virginia Creeper Trail, popular with
cyclists, passes through it, as does the Appalachian Trail.

The NPS operates nine campgrounds
and three cabins in the area; contact park
headquarters (p75) for details. For food, load
up your picnic basket or your backpack in
Abingdon or Marion.

The best way to get to the trails and
campsites is by car. The skinny recreation
area runs roughly north–south, with I-81 to
the west and the Blue Ridge Parkway to the
east. The Tennessee and North Carolina borders are nearby.

Heartwood ARTS CENTER
(📞 276-492-2400; www.myswva.org/heartwood;
1 Heartwood Circle; ⏰ 9am-5pm Mon-Wed, Fri &
Sat, to 9pm Thu, 10am-3pm Sun) Heartwood is
a showcase of regional crafts, cuisine, wine,
craft beer and traditional music. There are
exhibition spaces, retail galleries, a restaurant (sandwiches, salads, quiche) and a
brew bar. Don't miss Thursday nights, when
bluegrass bands and barbecue draw a festive
local crowd. It's about 3 miles east of town,
off Hwy 11.

Virginia Creeper Trail CYCLING, HIKING
(www.vacreepertrail.com) This 33.4-mile cycling
and hiking trail on an old railroad corridor
rolls through the Mount Rogers National

Barter Theatre, Abingdon

Recreation Area, connecting lofty Whitetop with Damascus and eventually Abingdon. Local bike companies rent out bikes and provide shuttle services.

Sleeping

Alpine Motel
MOTEL **$**

(☎ 276-628-3178; www.alpinemotelabingdon.com; 882 E Main St; r $49-69; P ❄ 🛜) Low room rates are the only reason to consider this somewhat depressing option on the highway east of the historic center. Large and musty rooms have wheezing air-con units and 1970s-era bathrooms. A basic breakfast is included.

Martha Washington Inn & Spa
HOTEL **$$$**

(☎ 276-628-3161; www.themartha.com; 150 W Main St; r $175-265, ste $385-595; P ❄ @ 🛜 🏊) This is the region's best-known historic hotel, a handsome Victorian-era hulk set amid formal gardens. The rocking chairs on the front porch are a pleasant place to relax, as is the library with its open fire. Rooms are comfortable but faded; food in the restaurant could be a lot better. Rates include breakfast. A compulsory resort fee ($16 per room per night) is levied on top of the room rate.

Facilities include an indoor saltwater pool, Jacuzzi, gym, tennis courts and mini-golf.

Eating

128 Pecan
AMERICAN **$$**

(☎ 276-698-3159; www.128pecan.com; 128 Pecan St; lunch mains $9-12, dinner mains $18-23; ⏱ 11am-9pm Tue-Sat; 🛜) There's something for everyone on the huge menu at this local favorite, which serves up excellent sandwiches, tacos and heartier meat or seafood dishes. Sit inside or on the front veranda.

★ Rain
AMERICAN **$$$**

(☎ 276-739-2331; www.rainabingdon.com; 283 E Main St; lunch mains $9-10, dinner mains $18-32; ⏱ 11am-2pm & 4-9pm Tue-Sat Feb-Dec, reduced hr Jan; P) Culinary influences here roam from Mexico, Asia and Mediterranean Europe but arrive with aplomb in contemporary America. The food is excellent, and extremely well priced for its quality, especially at lunch. Service is attentive and the lounge bar stays open after meals service. Good one.

Tavern
INTERNATIONAL **$$$**

(☎ 276-628-1118; www.abingdontavern.com; 222 E Main St; mains $22-44; ⏱ 5-9pm Mon-Sat) Serving meals to travellers since its establishment in 1779 (it's the oldest building in town), this place has a suitably old-fashioned menu and vibe. Dine on German specialities such as Wiener schnitzel, or on dishes including fillet mignon, crab cakes and rack of lamb. Vegetarians should steer clear.

🍷 Drinking & Entertainment

Wolf Hills Brewing Co   MICROBREWERY
(📞276-451-5470; www.wolfhillsbrewing.com; 350
Park St; ⏰5-8pm Mon-Fri, from 1pm Sat, 1-5pm
Sun) For satisfying microbrews and the occa-
sional live music session, head to Wolf Hills
Brewing Co.

Barter Theatre   THEATER
(📞276-628-3991; www.bartertheatre.com; 127 W
Main St; ⏰box office 9am-5pm Tue-Sat, from 1pm
Sun) Founded during the Depression, Barter
Theatre earned its name from audiences
trading food for performances. Actors Gregory Peck and Ernest Borgnine cut their teeth
on Barter's stage.

🛍 Shopping

**Holston Mountain
Artisans Shop**   ARTS & CRAFTS
(📞276-628-7721; www.holstonmtnarts.org; 214
Park St SE; ⏰10am-5pm Mon-Sat Apr-Dec, Thu-Sat

Mar, Fri & Sat Jan & Feb) Representing 150 local
craftspeople, this not-for-profit cooperative
is a great place to source pottery, jewellery,
patchwork, knitting, soap, pickles and other
artisanal items.

ℹ Information

Convention & Visitors Bureau (📞276-676-
2282; www.visitabingdonvirginia.com; 335
Cumming St) Supplies brochures including a
self-guided walking tour of Abingdon's historic
center. Also has a restroom.

ℹ Getting There & Away

Abingdon borders I-81 near the Virginia–
Tennessee border. The city is about 180 miles
northwest of Charlotte, NC. Regional airports
include Asheville Regional Airport (p95) in
Asheville, NC, and Roanoke-Blacksburg Regional
Airport (p77) in Roanoke.

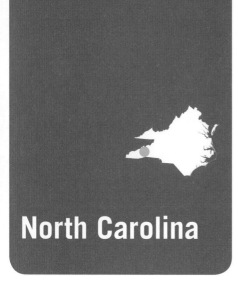

North Carolina

North Carolina combines the Old and the New South with outdoor adventures aplenty. Like in neighbouring Virginia, there are plenty of craft breweries to quench your thirst here too.

The rural, conservative Old South and the urban, liberal-leaning New South jostle for precedence in the fast-growing Tar Heel State, home to hipsters, hog farmers and high-tech wunderkinds. From the mighty mountains in the west to the ethereal islands lining the Atlantic coast, all kinds of cultures and communities manage to coexist.

The locals are joined, especially in summer, by visitors from around the world. Many are drawn by the limitless opportunities for adventures, including hiking the woods, rafting the rivers and cruising the Blue Ridge Parkway in a convertible. Others come to savor the dynamic cities, from Asheville in the mountains to Wilmington by the coast, with their wide-ranging attractions and top-notch restaurants – and astonishing number of craft breweries.

History

The tides of history have flowed back and forth across North Carolina. For Native Americans, the fragile coastline fringed the periphery of their world; for European colonizers, it marked the point from which they steadily pushed the original inhabitants westwards. Once it became part of the United States, North Carolina's fortunes became entwined with the plantation South, and it eventually seceded to join the Confederacy. Since then, the state has continued to identify with the South, while industrializing and entering the global economy.

❶ Information

Visit North Carolina (www.visitnc.com) The state's official tourism office puts out good maps and information, including its annual *Official Travel Guide*.

North Carolina State Parks (www.ncparks. gov) Offers info on North Carolina's 41 state parks and recreation areas, many of which have camping facilities.

❶ Getting There & Away

North Carolina's main gateways include Charlotte Douglas International Airport (p116) and **Raleigh-Durham International Airport** (RDU; ☑ 919-840-2123; www.rdu.com; 1000 Trade Dr, Morrisville). Smaller regional airports serve Asheville, Wilmington and, to a lesser extent, the southern Outer Banks and Crystal Coast. Amtrak and Greyhound are more prevalent in metropolitan areas.

NORTH CAROLINA MOUNTAINS

Towering along the skyline of western North Carolina, the mighty Appalachian Mountains hold several distinct subranges, among which the Great Smoky, Blue Ridge, Pisgah and Black Mountain ranges are especially dramatic. Carpeted in blue-green hemlock, pine and oak trees – logged a century ago but now preserved and protected – these cool hills are home to cougars,

View of Grandfather Mountain (p46)

deer, black bears, wild turkeys and great horned owls. For adventurous travelers, the potential for hiking, camping, climbing and rafting expeditions is all but endless, while yet another photo opportunity lies around every bend.

The Cherokee who hunted on these forested slopes were later joined by 18th-century Scots-Irish immigrants looking for a better life. Lofty towns such as Blowing Rock enticed the sickly, lured by the fresh mountain air. Today, scenic drives, leafy trails and roaring rivers draw visitors from around the world.

🛈 Getting There & Away

Asheville Regional Airport (p95) is the gateway to the North Carolina mountains, with nonstop flights to/from Atlanta, Charlotte, Chicago and New York, among others. Asheville also has a Greyhound (p95) station.

High Country

The northwestern corner of North Carolina, flanking the Blue Ridge Parkway as it sets off across the state from Virginia, is known as the High Country. Of the main towns, Boone is a lively college community that's home to Appalachian State University (ASU), while Blowing Rock and Banner Elk are quaint tourist centers near the winter ski areas.

🛈 Information

Blowing Rock's High Country Regional Welcome Center (p86) can advise on accommodations and outdoors outfitters.

🛈 Getting There & Away

The High Country is an easy drive from Asheville or Charlotte, with Charlotte Douglas International Airport (p116) the closest air gateway.

Boone

🕿 828 / POP 18,834

Boone is a fun and lively mountain town where the predominantly youthful inhabitants – many of them students at bustling Appalachian State University – share a hankering for the outdoors. Renowned for its bluegrass musicians and Appalachian storytellers, the town is named after pioneer and explorer Daniel Boone, who often camped in the area. Downtown Boone features a fine assortment of low-rise brick-broad, Colonial Revival, art deco and streamline-modern buildings. Those that line King St in particular now tend to house charming boutiques, cafes, and crafts galleries. The hamlet of Valle Crucis is eight miles west.

Every summer since 1952, local history has been presented in a dramatization called *Horn in the West,* performed in an outdoor amphitheater above town.

◉ Sights

Foggy Mountain Gem Mine   MINE
(p45)

Doc Watson Statue   STATUE
(p45)

✨ Festivals & Events

**Appalachian
Summer Festival**   PERFORMING ARTS
(www.appsummer.org; ⊙ Jul–early Aug) This prestigious month-long arts showcase, staged by Boone's Appalachian State University, uses venues all over campus, and centers on the Schaefer Center for the Performing Arts. Originally rooted in classical music, it now extends across theater, film and the visual arts.

👉 Tours

River & Earth Adventures   ADVENTURE
(☑ 828-355-9797; www.raftcavehike.com; 6201 Castle Ford Rd, Todd; half-/full-day rafting $60/100; 🚣) Eco-conscious operators offering everything from family-friendly caving trips to rafting class V rapids at Watauga Gorge – plus organic lunches! Canoe ($65), kayak ($35 to $65) and tube ($20) rentals are offered too.

🛏 Sleeping

Accommodations in Boone traditionally consisted of standard chain hotels, but the Horton, downtown's first boutique hotel, opened in 2018. You can also find the occasional historic B&B, rental farmhouse or cozy log cabin around town and in the surrounding countryside.

Hidden Valley Motel   MOTEL $
(☑ 828-963-4372; www.hiddenvalleymotel.com; 8725 Hwy 105 S; r from $62; P🐾) A quintessential mom-n-pop motel, set in delightful flower-filled gardens 8 miles southwest of town. The main house is bursting with vintage charm, while the eight guest rooms are cozy but plainer.

Lovill House Inn   B&B $$
(☑ 828-264-4204; www.lovillhouseinn.com; 404 Old Bristol Rd; r from $179; 🐾) Boone's finest B&B is a splendid 19th-century farmhouse, a mile west of downtown and surrounded by woods. With its snug rooms, white clapboard walls, and wraparound porch decked out with rocking chairs, it's all wonderfully restful; the breakfast is worth getting up for, though.

Mast Farm Inn   B&B $$
(☑ 828-963-5857; www.themastfarminn.com; 2543 Broadstone Rd, Valle Crucis; r/cottage from $169/299; P🌸🐾) Featuring worn hardwood floors, claw-foot tubs, and handmade toffees on your bedside table, this restored farmhouse in the beautiful hamlet of Valle Crucis epitomizes rustic chic. Nine cabins and cottages are also available. Settle into the 1806 Loom House log cabin, fire up the wood-burning fireplace and never leave.

As well as breakfast, rates include an evening happy hour with local cheeses and sweets.

Horton Hotel   BOUTIQUE HOTEL $$
(☑ 828-832-8060; www.thehorton.com; 611 W King St; r from $189; 🌸🐾) The 2018 opening of this ultra-central 15-room boutique hotel, in what was once a Studebaker showroom, adds a welcome dash of contemporary style to Boone's lodging options. Its open-air rooftop is a wonderful vantage point overlooking downtown.

🍴 Eating & Drinking

Thanks largely to its many students, Boone holds the High Country's biggest concentration of restaurants. There's plenty of choice, ranging from Southern US to Latin American.

Wild Craft Eatery   LATIN AMERICAN $
(☑ 828-262-5000; www.wildcrafteatery.com; 506 W King St; mains $11-14; ⊙ 11am-10pm Tue-Sun; 🍴) Colorful, quirky downtown cafe, with an outdoor deck on King St, and an emphasis on local ingredients. There's a definite Latin flavor to the menu, with tacos and tamales aplenty, but they also offer Thai noodles and shepherd's pie. Not everything's vegetarian, but most of the standout dishes are, including the Cuzco Cakes, made with smoked quinoa, Gouda and yams.

Melanie's Food Fantasy   CAFE $
(☑ 828-263-0300; www.melaniesfoodfantasy.com; 664 W King St; breakfast mains $6-13, lunch & dinner mains $9-18; ⊙ 8:30am-2pm Sun-Wed, to 9pm Thu-Sat; 🍴) Students and hippie types gather at this farm-to-fork favorite – out on the patio, for much of the year – to gobble serious breakfast dishes (scrambles, eggs Benedict, omelets, pancakes) with a side of home fries. Later on, there's excellent creative Southern cuisine (chipotle-honey salmon and grits, blackened pimiento-cheese burger), with vegetarian options always available (tempeh, soysage etc).

Dan'l Boone Inn SOUTHERN US **$$**
(📞 828-264-8657; www.danlbooneinn.com; 130 Hardin St; breakfast adult $12, child $5-9, lunch & dinner adult $19, child $6-12; ⊙ 11:30am-8:30pm Mon-Thu, from 8am Fri-Sun, dinner only Sat & Sun Nov-May; 🛜🍽️) Quantity is the name of the game at this restaurant, where the family-style meals are a Boone (sorry) for hungry hikers. Everyone pays the same price, and you can eat as much fried chicken and steak (lunch and dinner) or ham, sausage and bacon (breakfast) as you like. No credit cards.

Cardinal CRAFT BEER
(📞 828-366-9600; www.thecardinalboone.com; 1711 Hwy 105; ⊙ 11am-midnight Mon-Thu, to 2am Fri & Sat, noon-midnight Sun; 🛜) Locals hunker down in this cozy, barn-like space, 2 miles south of downtown, for Boone's best range of local and regional craft beer (pints $5) – 12 taps in all, as well as $10 craft cocktails. You can also enjoy excellent farm-driven burgers (beef, beet, bison, or game) and pinball or Skee-Ball.

🛍️ Shopping

**Original Mast
General Store** SPORTS & OUTDOORS
(p44)

**Original Mast
General Store Annex** SPORTS & OUTDOORS
(www.mastgeneralstore.com; Hwy 194, Valle Crucis; ⊙ 10am-6pm Mon-Sat, from noon Sun) Boone's

nearby Mast General Store took over this former rival in Valle Crucis way back when, and now stocks it with outdoor apparel, hiking gear and a whole lot of candy.

ℹ️ Getting There & Away

The closest commercial airport to Boone is Charlotte Douglas International Airport (p116), 94 miles southeast.

Blowing Rock

📞 828 / POP 1288

A stately and idyllic mountain village, tiny Blowing Rock beckons from its perch at 4000ft above sea level, the only full-service town directly on the Blue Ridge Parkway. It's easy to be seduced by its postcard-perfect Main St, lined with antique shops, kitschy boutiques, potters, silversmiths, sweet shops, lively taverns and excellent restaurants. There are even a couple of bucolic, duck-filled lakes to drive home the storybook nature of it all. The only thing that spoils the illusion is the sheer difficulty of finding a place to park in high season.

◉ Sights

Blowing Rock makes a homier base than nearby Boone, 8 miles north, for High Country attractions such as the Tweetsie Railroad (p46), North Carolina's only remaining fully functional steam-engine train, and Grandfather Mountain (p46). As you drive in, pick

ELIZABETH ABALO / SHUTTERSTOCK ©

Scenery around Blowing Rock

up a historic downtown walking-tour map from the regional welcome center (☏828-264-1299; www.highcountryhost.com; 6370 Hwy 321 S; ⊙9am-5pm Mon-Sat, to 3pm Sun).

🛏 Sleeping & Eating

Cliff Dwellers Inn MOTEL $
(☏828-414-9596; www.cliffdwellers.com; 116 Lakeview Terrace; r/apt from $124/144; ❄🛜🐾) From its perch above town, this aptly named motel entices guests with good service, reasonable prices, stylish rooms and balconies with sweeping vistas.

Green Park Inn HISTORIC HOTEL $$
(☏828-414-9230; www.greenparkinn.com; 9239 Valley Blvd; r $94-299; 🅿❄🛜🐾) This grand white clapboard hotel, 1 mile south of downtown, opened its doors in 1891, and was renovated in 2010 to hold 88 plush rooms and a grill restaurant. The eastern continental divide runs straight through the bar, and Margaret Mitchell stayed here while writing *Gone with the Wind*.

⭐ Bistro Roca AMERICAN $$
(☏828-295-4008; www.bistroroca.com; 143 Wonderland Trail; lunch mains $9-16, dinner mains $10-32; ⊙11am-3pm & 5-10pm Wed-Mon; 🛜) This cozy, lodge-like bistro, in a Prohibition-era building just off Main St, serves upscale New American cuisine – lobster or pork-belly mac and cheese, kicked-up habanero burgers, mountain-trout *banh mi* sandwiches – with an emphasis on local everything. Check out the walls of the atmospheric Antlers Bar, North Carolina's longest continually operating bar, plastered with fantastic B&W pet photos.

Savannah's Oyster House SEAFOOD $$
(☏828-414-9354; www.savannahoysterhouse.com; 155 Sunset Dr; mains $10-32; ⊙11am-9pm Tue-Thu & Sun, to 10pm Fri & Sat; 🛜) Get over the weirdness of finding a Low Country seafood place in the High Country – let alone the giant shark hanging in the stairwell – and there's much to like about this little cottage restaurant. There's the oysters, obviously, but also the sumptuous, cheesy shrimp 'n' grits, and the varied menu of seafood boils, fish 'n' chips and lobster potpie.

🍺 Drinking & Nightlife

Blowing Rock Ale House MICROBREWERY
(☏828-414-9254; www.blowingrockbrewing.com; 152 Sunset Dr; ⊙11:30am-9pm Mon, Tue & Thu, to 10pm Fri & Sat, noon-9pm Sun; 🛜) Blowing Rock's first craft brewery offers 12 taps of locally produced suds (pints $5), including a popular pilsner, DIPA and chocolate porter, in a 1940s lodge house.

There's food as well as five rooms upstairs ($175), so you don't have to stumble far – though those stairs could be tricky!

🔒 Shopping

Parkway Craft Center ARTS & CRAFTS
(☏828-295-7938; www.southernhighlandguild.org; Mile 294, Blue Ridge Pkwy, Moses H Cone Memorial Park; ⊙9am-5pm mid-Mar–Nov) The Parkway Craft Center, where the Southern Highland Craft Guild sells superb crafts, is housed in a 1901 Colonial Revival mansion that's directly accessible from the parkway and also holds a small museum (p46).

ℹ Getting There & Away

Blowing Rock is 8 miles south of Boone via Hwy 321, or more like 25 miles if you detour along the Blue Ridge Parkway. The nearest commercial airport is Charlotte Douglas International Airport (p116), 87 miles southeast.

Asheville

☏828 / POP 89,121

The undisputed 'capital' of the North Carolina mountains, Asheville is both a major tourist destination and one of the coolest small cities in the South. Cradled in a sweeping curve of the Blue Ridge Parkway, it offers easy access to outdoor adventures of all kinds, while downtown's historic art deco buildings hold stylish New Southern restaurants, decadent chocolate shops, and the homegrown microbreweries that explain the nickname 'Beer City.'

Despite rapid gentrification, Asheville remains recognizably an overgrown mountain town that holds tight to its traditional roots. It's also a rare liberal enclave in the conservative countryside, home to a sizable population of artists and hard-core hippies. Alternative Asheville life is largely lived in neighborhoods such as the waterfront River Arts District and, across the French Broad River, West Asheville. Remarkably enough, the French Broad River is the world's third-oldest river, its course laid before life on Earth even began.

◎ Sights & Activities

Downtown Asheville, which still looks much as it must have in the 1930s, is compact and

Asheville

Asheville

◎ Sights

✪ Activities, Courses & Tours

🛏 Sleeping

🍴 Eating

🍷 Drinking & Nightlife

✪ Entertainment

🛍 Shopping

easy to negotiate on foot. Apart perhaps from its breweries, the city's best-known attraction is the grandiose Biltmore Estate (p49), the largest privately owned home in the country. It luxuriates across a vast green expanse that stretches from Biltmore Village, 2.4 miles south of downtown.

Asheville Pinball Museum
MUSEUM

(Map p87; ☑ 828-776-5671; http://ashevillepinball. com; 1 Battle Sq; adult/child 5-10yr $15/12; ⊘ 1-6pm Mon & Sun, 2-9pm Wed-Fri, noon-9pm Sat) A veritable time machine, this downtown treat transports gamers back to the much-lamented pinball arcades of yesteryear. With stock ranging from vintage cowboy-and-Indian games up to brand-new Game of Thrones editions, something is certain to flip your flippers. Your admission fee covers unlimited plays, though you may have to wait your turn on popular machines.

Folk Art Center
CULTURAL CENTER

(p48)

Chimney Rock Park
PARK

(p50)

Asheville Art Museum
MUSEUM

(Map p87; ☑ 828-253-3227; www.ashevilleart.org; 2 S Pack Sq) Asheville is waiting with bated breath for the 2019 reopening of its art museum. A huge construction project has been transforming and expanding its Pack Sq home to double the space available for its permanent collection and short-term special exhibitions.

aSHEville Museum
MUSEUM

(Map p87; ☑ 828-785-5722; www.ashevillemu seum.com; 35 Wall St; admission by donation, from $5; ⊘ 10am-10pm Sun-Thu, to 11pm Fri & Sat, shorter hr Nov-May) Who put the 'she' in Asheville? This dynamic downtown museum, where changing 'her-story' exhibits celebrate the achievements of women and girls the world over. There's an emphasis on local heroines such as Wilma Dykeman, whose 1955 book *The French Broad* decried the polluting of Asheville's principal river.

Thomas Wolfe Memorial
HOUSE

(Map p87; ☑ 828-253-8304; www.wolfememo rial.com; 52 N Market St; museum free, house tour adult/child 7-17yr $5/2; ⊘ 9am-5pm Tue-Sat) An incongruous survivor of old Asheville, this downtown clapboard structure was the childhood home of *Look Homeward, Angel* author Thomas Wolfe (1900–38). His autobiographical 1929 novel so offended locals that he didn't return to Asheville (which he fictionalized as 'Altamont') for eight years. Hourly tours, on the half-hour, enter the house itself.

Smoky Mountain Adventure Center
OUTDOORS

(Map p89; ☑ 828-505-4446; www.smacasheville. com; 173 Amboy Rd; ⊘ 8am-8pm Mon, to 10pm Tue-Sat, 10am-8pm Sun) One-stop adventure shopping, across the French Broad River 3 miles southwest of downtown. On-site there's an indoor climbing wall, as well as yoga and tai chi classes. They can also arrange bikes for the Blue Ridge Parkway, inner-tubes and paddleboards for the river, plus guided rock climbing, backpacking, day hiking, ice climbing and mountaineering trips.

☞ Tours

BREW-ed
BREWERY

(Map p87; ☑ 828-278-9255; www.brew-ed.com; adults $37-50, nondrinkers $20) Beer-focused historical walking tours, led by Cicerone-certified beer geeks and sampling at two or three different downtown breweries, on Thursdays (5:30pm), Fridays (2pm), Saturdays (11:30am and 2pm) and Sundays (1pm).

Lazoom Tours
BUS

(Map p87; ☑ 828-225-6932; www.lazoomtours. com; $23-29) For a hysterical historical tour of the city, hop on the purple bus, watch out for nuns on bikes – and bring your own booze. Weekend tours feature a live band and stop at breweries.

★★ Festivals & Events

★ Mountain Dance & Folk Festival
MUSIC

(☑ 828-258-6101; www.folkheritage.org; AB Tech/Mission Health Conference Center, 340 Victoria Rd; 1/3 nights $25/60; ⊘ 1st Thu-Sat Aug; ♿) North Carolina's premier showcase for old-time music, this three-day bonanza was founded in 1928 by banjo and fiddle player Bascom Lamar Lansford, as the first folk festival in the entire country.

Craft Fair of the Southern Highlands
ART

(☑ 828-298-7928; www.southernhighlandguild.org; US Cellular Center, 87 Haywood St; ⊘ 3rd weekend Jul & Oct) At these two three-day annual fairs, craftworkers from all over the South gather to display and sell traditional and contemporary work in all media, including clay, metal, wood, glass and paper.

Greater Asheville

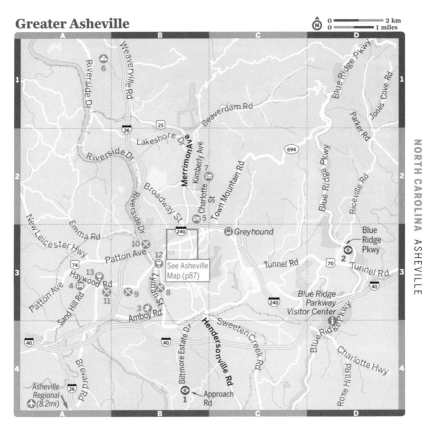

🛏 Sleeping

If you want to be within walking distance of shops, restaurants and South Slope's breweries, downtown is the best place to stay. It holds very few inexpensive options, however. Victorian-style B&Bs are concentrated in the historic Montford neighborhood, a mile north, while chain motels are mostly further out still. The **Asheville Bed & Breakfast Association** (☑ 828-250-0200; www.asheville bba.com) handles bookings for a dozen local inns and B&Bs, from gingerbread cottages to alpine lodges.

⭐ **Sweet Peas Hostel**　　　　HOSTEL $
(Map p87; ☑ 828-285-8488; www.sweetpeas hostel.com; 23 Rankin Ave; dm/pod $32/40, r without/with bath $75/105; ❄ @ 🖱) This spick-and-span, well-run, contemporary hostel occupies an unbeatable downtown location. The loft-like open-plan space, with its exposed brick walls, steel bunks and blond-wood sleeping

Greater Asheville

⊙ Sights

⊕ Activities, Courses & Tours

🛏 Sleeping

⊗ Eating

⊙ Drinking & Nightlife

Omni Grove Park Inn, Asheville

'pods', can get noisy, but at least there's a 10% discount at the Lexington Ave Brewery downstairs. They also warn you if an event coincides with your planned dates.

Downtown Inn & Suites   MOTEL $

(Map p87; ☑ 828-254-9661; www.downtowninnandsuites.com; 120 Patton Ave; r $95; P 🛜) The Downtown Inn will only suit those who value location and price above amenities and peace. It's an old-style motel on a noisy street, with old-fashioned rooms, but they're reasonably sized and cozy, and you won't find a better price – or free parking, for that matter – elsewhere in the heart of downtown. Rates include a simple buffet breakfast.

Asheville Glamping   TENTED CAMP $

(☑ 828-450-9745; www.ashevilleglamping.com; trailer/yurt/tipi/dome from $100/120/125/135, plus room-cleaning fee per stay $50; 🛜) Friendly Joana runs three separate sites: two within 5 miles of downtown, the other 10 miles north towards Hot Springs. Each is peppered with a combination of glammed-up yurts, domes, tipis and vintage Airstream and Spartan trailers, some equipped with hot tubs, deluxe outdoor gas grills and prime Blue Ridge views. There's a minimum stay of two nights. You'll need to be self-sufficient, but for a certain kind of traveler this is a unique getaway.

Bon Paul & Sharky's   HOSTEL $

(Map p89; ☑ 828-775-3283; www.bonpaulandsharkys.com; 816 Haywood Rd; tent sites per person $21.40, dm/r from $30/78, cottage $105; P @ 🛜 🐾) Bon Paul & Sharky's has been welcoming hostelers into this colorful West Asheville 1920 home, a $10 Uber ride from South Slope, for well over a decade. There's also a separate cottage, while campers in the garden share the bathrooms indoors. Plenty of good bars and restaurants lie within shouting distance (plus an organic market), or you can BYOB.

Campfire Lodgings   CAMPGROUND $$

(Map p89; ☑ 828-658-8012; www.campfirelodgings.com; 116 Appalachian Village Rd; tent sites $35-40, RV sites $50-70, yurts $115-135, cabins $160; P 🛜 🐾) All yurts should have flat-screen TVs, don't you think? Sleep like the world's most stylish Mongolian nomad in a furnished multiroom tent, half a mile up a wooded hillside on an unpaved but passable road, 6 miles north of town. Cabins and tent sites are also available. RV sites, higher up, enjoy stunning valley views and the only wi-fi access.

★ Bunn House   BOUTIQUE HOTEL $$$

(Map p89; ☑ 828-333-8700; www.bunnhouse.com; 15 Clayton St; d $249-424; P ❄ 🛜) The six rooms and suites in this meticulously restored 1905 home, in a residential neighborhood half a mile north of downtown, are awash with exposed brick and dark hardwoods. The small rooftop terrace boasts Blue Ridge vistas, while the heated bathroom floors and subway-tiled steam showers are glorious on chilly mountain mornings.

There's no on-site reception – it's like having your own amazing studio apartment. Age 21 and over only.

Aloft Asheville Downtown   HOTEL $$$

(Map p87; 828-232-2838; www.aloftasheville downtown.com; 51 Biltmore Ave; r from $289; P❄@🛜🏊🐾) With a giant chalkboard in the lobby, groovy young staff, and an outdoor clothing store on the 1st floor, this place looks like the inner circle of hipster. The only thing missing is a wool-cap-wearing bearded guy drinking a hoppy microbrew – oh wait, over there. We jest. Once settled, you'll find the staff knowledgeable and the rooms colorful and spacious.

Not only is the hotel close to several downtown hot spots, its W XYZ bar hosts live music Thursday, Friday and Saturday.

Omni Grove Park Inn   HISTORIC HOTEL $$$

(Map p89; 828-252-2711; www.omnihotels.com; 290 Macon Ave; r $149-419; P❄@🛜🏊🐾) Commanding sweeping Blue Ridge views, this titanic Arts and Crafts–style stone lodge harks back to a bygone era of mountain glamor. Each of the 36ft-wide lobby fireplaces can hold a standing grown man, and has its own elevator to the chimney. Beyond the spectacular public spaces, though, the guest rooms can seem small by modern standards.

As well as a gargantuan underground spa, with stone pools and indoor waterfalls (day pass $90), the hotel has a golf course, indoor and outdoor tennis courts, and a 'base camp' for the Nantahala Outdoor Center (p100).

✕ Eating

★12 Bones   BARBECUE $

(Map p89; 828-253-4499; www.12bones.com; 5 Foundy St; dishes $5.50-22.50; 11am-4pm Mon-Fri) How good is the barbecue at 12 Bones? Good enough to lure the vacationing Barack and Michelle Obama back to the River Arts District, a few years back. Expect a long wait, though, before you get to enjoy the slow-cooked, smoky and tender meats, or succulent sides from jalapeño-cheese grits to smoked potato salad.

The warehouse-like space is shared with an outlet of Wedge Brewing (p93); in-the-know regulars skip the line by picking up food from the take-out counter and carrying it around to the pub.

Chai Pani   INDIAN $

(Map p87; 828-254-4003; www.chaipaniashe ville.com; 22 Battery Park Ave; snacks $6.50-10, meals $12; 11:30am-3:30pm & 5-9:30pm; 🖐) Literally 'tea and water,' chai pani refers more generally to inexpensive snacks. Hence the ever-changing array of irresistible street food at this popular, no-reservations downtown restaurant. Fill up on crunchy bhel puri (chickpea noodles and puffed rice) or live it larger with a lamb burger, fish roll, or chicken or vegetarian thali (a full meal on a metal tray).

Buxton Hall   BARBECUE $

(Map p87; 828-232-7216; www.buxtonhall.com; 32 Banks Ave; mains $12-21; 11:30am-3pm & 5:30-10pm; 🖐) What happens when two James Beard–nominated chefs, Meherwan Irani and Elliott Moss, open a whole-hog barbecue joint in a cavernous former skating rink on the South Slope? You get the ridiculously good buttermilk-fried-chicken sandwich at Buxton Hall, that's what.

Eastern Carolina–style barbecue here is smoked slow and low – that's the tempo – for 18 hours over hardwood coals, infused with a Moss-family vinegar mop. Everything is mouthwateringly unforgettable – including the key lime pie, summed up by our server as 'stupid.' No reservations.

Sunny Point Cafe   CAFE $

(Map p89; 828-252-0055; www.sunnypoint cafe.com; 626 Haywood Rd; breakfast dishes $6-12, mains $10-19; 8am-2:30pm Sun & Mon, to 9:30pm Tue-Sat) 🍽 Loved for its hearty homemade food, this bright West Asheville spot fills up each morning with solos, couples and ladies who breakfast; the little garden out front is the prime spot. Everything, waitstaff included, embraces the organic and fresh. The insanely good huevos rancheros, oozing feta cheese and chorizo sausage, should come with an instruction manual, while the biscuits are divine.

French Broad
Chocolate Lounge   DESSERTS $

(Map p87; 828-252-4181; www.frenchbroadcho colates.com; 10 S Pack Sq; desserts $2.75-7.50; 11am-11pm Sun-Thu, to midnight Fri & Sat) Now happily ensconced in large, glossy premises beside Pack Sq Park, this beloved downtown chocolate shop hasn't lost its chocolate heart. Small-batch, locally produced organic chocolates, chunky chocolate brownies, chocolate-dipped ginger cookies, a sippable 'liquid truffle'…hey, where'd you go?

White Duck Taco Shop   MEXICAN $

(Map p87; 828-232-9191; www.whiteducktaco shop.com; 12 Biltmore Ave; tacos $3.45-5.25;

⊙11:30am-9pm Mon-Sat, 10:30am-3pm Sun) The chalkboard menu at this downtown taco shop will give you fits. Every single one of these hefty soft tacos sounds like a must-have flavor bomb: spicy buffalo chicken with blue-cheese sauce, crispy pork belly, mole-roasted duck – even shrimp and grits! The margaritas are mighty fine too.

In the River Arts District, stop by 1 Roberts St, their original location.

Early Girl Eatery   CAFE $

(Map p87; ☑828-259-9292; www.earlygirleatery.com; 8 Wall St; mains $5-16; ⊙7:30am-3pm Mon-Wed, to 9pm Thu & Fri, 8am-9pm Sat & Sun) It's the all-day breakfast menu that draws the crowds to this downtown farm-to-table cafe, where the sunny dining room overlooks a small central square. Go for the house Benny, with tomato, spinach, avocado and poached eggs on grit cakes, or a grilled pimiento-cheese sandwich if it's past your breakfast time.

★ Cúrate   TAPAS $$

(Map p87; ☑828-239-2946; www.curatetapasbar.com; 13 Biltmore Ave; small plates $6-18; ⊙11:30am-10:30pm Tue-Fri, from 10am Sat & Sun) ✐ Owned by hip Ashevillian chef Katie Button and her Catalan husband Félix, this convivial downtown hangout celebrates the simple charms and sensual flavors of Spanish tapas, while adding an occasional Southern twist. Standout dishes run long and wide: *pan con tomate* (grilled bread with tomato), lightly fried eggplant drizzled with honey and rosemary, and a knockout squid-ink 'paella' with vermicelli.

It also features a Barcelona-style *vermuteria* (vermouth bar). Savor the flavors, order another glass of Garnacha and converse with your dinner companions, not your phone. Reservations are a must, especially on weekends, but you can usually snag a bar seat fairly quickly after 9pm.

Smoky Park Supper Club   AMERICAN $$

(Map p89; ☑828-350-0315; www.smokypark.com; 350 Riverside Dr; mains $13-36; ⊙5-9pm Tue-Thu, 4-10pm Fri & Sat, 10:30am-9pm Sun; 🐾) An anchor of cool in the River Arts District, the largest container-constructed restaurant in the USA is more than the sum of its parts – 19 shipping containers to be exact. Choose between such wood-fired delights as garlic- and lemon-roasted half chicken, cast-iron-seared Carolina fish, or, for vegetarians, roasted local apples stuffed with kale, walnuts and smoked cheddar.

Tupelo Honey   SOUTHERN US $$

(Map p87; ☑828-255-4863; www.tupelohoneycafe.com; 12 College St; brunch mains $6-17, lunch & dinner mains $9.50-30; ⊙9am-9pm Sun-Thu, to 10pm Fri & Sat) The flagship downtown location of this Asheville-based chain is renowned for New Southern favorites, such as shrimp and grits with goat's cheese – even if the Tupelo-born Elvis himself would surely have gone for the fried-chicken BLT with apple-cider bacon! Brunches are superb, but no matter the meal, say yes to the biscuit. And add a drop of honey.

Admiral   AMERICAN $$$

(Map p89; ☑828-252-2541; www.theadmiralasheville.com; 400 Haywood Rd; small plates $12-18, large plates $30-38; ⊙5-10pm; 🐾) Set in a concrete bunker beside a car junkyard, this low-key West Asheville spot looks divey from the outside. It's inside, though, where the magic happens. One of the state's finest New American restaurants, the Admiral serves wildly creative dishes – saffron tagliatelle with lima beans, zucchini and basil pesto, for example – that taste divine.

🍷 Drinking & Nightlife

Asheville is the craft-beer capital of the South, only rivaled in quality and quantity across the entire USA by Portland's Oregon and Maine. The live-music scene is extremely vibrant: you can find music nightly, with bluegrass and old-time aplenty but much more besides; and the Asheville Symphony Orchestra is very progressive, collaborating with hip-hop acts etc.

★ Burial   MICROBREWERY

(Map p87; www.burialbeer.com; 40 Collier Ave; ⊙2-10pm Mon-Thu, from noon Fri-Sun; 🐾) This ever-progressive brewery gives experimental batches of Belgian-leaning styles – farmhouse saisons, strong dubbels and tripels – a Southern kick in the pants, using local ingredients such as wildflower honey, chokeberries and juniper branches. Brewers in overalls, a menacing logo, and pitchfork-and-sickle tap and door handles add intrigue. It takes significant willpower to leave the outdoor patio. There's a decent food menu too.

★ Funkatorium   MICROBREWERY

(Map p87; ☑828-552-3203; www.wickedweedbrewing.com/locations/funkatorium; 147 Coxe Ave; ⊙2-10pm Mon-Thu, noon-midnight Fri & Sat, 11am-10pm Sun; 🐾) If you need the funk, you gotta have that funk…and you'll find it at the

BEER CITY USA

If ever a city was transformed by the craft-beer movement, it's Asheville. A sleepy mountain city when its first brewery, Highland Brewing, opened in 1994, Asheville has become a true destination city for booze-bent hopheads. It now holds almost 30 breweries, catering to a population of around 90,000 locals; were it not for the half a million tourists who join them each year, that would be a lot of beer per person!

Inevitably, big-name national breweries have been flocking to Asheville too. Both New Belgium and Sierra Nevada, respectively from California and Colorado, have opened major brewing and taproom facilities here. Strolling from brewery to beerhouse in the pub-packed South Slope district – which, yes, slopes south from downtown – it's easy to see why Asheville has been nicknamed Beer City.

Stop by the visitor center or ask your hotel for the free *Field Guide to Breweries*, which provides key details and maps for the Asheville Ale Trail (www.ashevillealetrail.com), an association of local breweries, taprooms and pubs that organizes tours and events.

East Coast's first taproom dedicated to sour, wild ale, Brett and funky beer. For fans, it's pilgrimage-worthy. The rough-and-ready, old world–style taproom holds more than 600 aging barrels, and rotating taps spit 8oz pours for the cause. Get funked up!

Battery Park Book Exchange & Champagne Bar WINE BAR
(Map p87; ☑ 828-252-0020; www.batteryparkbookexchange.com; 1 Page Ave; ◷ 11am-9pm Sun-Thu, to 10pm Fri & Sat) A charming champagne bar, sprawling through several opulent vintage-furnished rooms of a glorious old downtown shopping arcade, with every nook and cranny lined with shelves of neatly cataloged secondhand books covering every imaginable topic. Seriously, who could resist that as a combination? Other wines are also available, along with coffee, cake, cheese and charcuterie.

Wedge Brewing MICROBREWERY
(Map p89; ☑ 828-505-2792; www.wedgebrewing.com; 37 Paynes Way; ◷ noon-10pm; 🐾) Unlike the spit-shined, well-oiled breweries elsewhere in Asheville, the grungier Wedge in the River Arts District is happy to keep things edgy. The beers are excellent – especially the Iron Rail IPA – but it's the fairy-lit outdoor patio, packed with convivial locals and their dogs, that gives it a one-up on fellow taprooms. Food trucks nightly.

Another outlet, nearby and also in the River Arts District, shares a space with 12 Bones (p91).

Wicked Weed MICROBREWERY
(Map p87; ☑ 828-575-9599; www.wickedweedbrewing.com; 91 Biltmore Ave; ◷ 11:30am-11pm Mon-Thu, to 1am Fri & Sat, noon-11pm Sun; 🐾) Henry VIII called hops 'a wicked and pernicious weed' that ruined the taste of beer. His subjects kept quaffing it anyway – just like the lively crowd in this former gas station, which overflows with hoppy brews. Equipped with 58 taps and a broad front patio, it's a big and breezy spot to chill.

Trade & Lore COFFEE
(Map p87; ☑ 828-424-7291; www.tradeandlore.com; 37 Wall St; ◷ 8am-7pm Tue-Thu, to 10pm Fri-Mon; 🐾) Deft baristas dole out serious java in this trendy downtown coffeehouse, drowning in industrial cool but leavened by occasional fits of vintage furniture. Espresso comes courtesy of a top-end La Marzocco machine, and there are four beer taps for lovers of another tipple.

The all-gender bathrooms are a tongue-in-cheek dig at state government.

Thirsty Monk CRAFT BEER
(Map p87; ☑ 828-254-5470; www.monkpub.com; 92 Patton Ave; ◷ 4pm-midnight Mon-Thu, noon-1:30am Fri & Sat, noon-10pm Sun) This scruffy but lovable downtown pub nails a fine drinking trifecta. Downstairs you'll find 16 taps and nearly 200 bottles of Belgian ales; at street level, 20 taps of proprietary, North Carolina and regional craft beers; and on the roof, craft cocktails dating back to before Prohibition.

O. Henry's GAY
(Map p87; ☑ 828-254-1891; www.ohenrysofasheville.com; 237 Haywood St; ◷ 4pm-3am) Open since 1976, North Carolina's longest-standing gay men's bar is an Asheville institution, with 'Take the Cake' karaoke on

Mast General Store, Asheville

Wednesdays – winners earn a fresh-baked cake – and drag at weekends. Its Underground dance bar, at the back, opens Friday and Saturday only.

Hi-Wire MICROBREWERY

(Map p87; ☑ 828-738-2448; www.hiwirebrewing.com; 197 Hilliard Ave; ⏲ 4-11pm Mon-Thu, 2pm-1am Fri, noon-1am Sat, 1-10pm Sun) Set in what used to be a mechanic's garage, this popular South Slope brewery offers a choice array of easy-drinking brews. Its taproom makes a mellow spot to hang with friends on a Saturday afternoon.

Westville Pub CRAFT BEER

(Map p89; ☑ 828-225-9782; www.westvillepub.com; 777 Haywood Rd; ⏲ 10:30am-2am) There's no better spot in West Asheville to bond with local 20- and 30-somethings, over a bottle or two of organic ale, than this veteran neighborhood bar.

☆ Entertainment

Orange Peel LIVE MUSIC

(Map p87; ☑ 828-398-1837; www.theorangepeel.net; 101 Biltmore Ave; tickets $10-35; ⏲ shows from 8pm) Asheville's premier live-music venue, downtown's Orange Peel Social Aid & Pleasure Club has been a showcase for big-name indie and punk bands since 2002. A warehouse-sized place, it seats – well, stands – a thousand-strong crowd.

🛍 Shopping

Horse & Hero ARTS & CRAFTS

(Map p87; ☑ 828-505-2133; www.facebook.com/horseandhero; 124 Patton Ave; ⏲ 11am-7pm Sun-Thu, to 9pm Fri & Sat) For a taste of Asheville's contemporary creativity, and a distinctly psychedelic take on Appalachian art, drop into this groovy downtown gallery. As well as graphic design pieces and lithographs, it sells plenty of more affordable craftwork.

Mast General Store SPORTS & OUTDOORS

(Map p87; ☑ 828-232-1883; www.mastgeneralstore.com; 15 Biltmore Ave; ⏲ 10am-6pm Mon-Thu, to 9pm Fri & Sat, noon-6pm Sun) This long-standing North Carolina favorite is great for outdoor gear, organic and natural cosmetics, provisions, candy, toys – you name it – much of it produced locally.

East Fork Pottery CERAMICS

(Map p87; ☑ 828-575-2150; www.eastforkpottery.com; 82 N Lexington Ave; ⏲ 11am-6pm Mon-Sat, noon-5pm Sun) Beautiful ceramic mugs and plates, made by a collective team of local ceramicists that includes Alex Matisse, the great-grandson of Henri himself. Their shop also sells a few of their favorite things, such as artisanal Japanese cutlery and nail clippers, and wonderful high-end handmade soaps.

Chocolate Fetish CHOCOLATE

(Map p87; ☑ 828-258-2353; www.chocolatefetish.com; 36 Haywood St; ⏲ 11am-7pm Mon-Thu, to 9pm Fri & Sat, noon-6pm Sun) With its silky truffles

($2.25) and sinfully good caramels, not to mention 20-minute tasting tours ($10), Chocolate Fetish deserves a flag on any chocolate addict's map. Recommendations? Chai Moon (chai tea and cinnamon), Mocha Magic (almond with espresso) and, our favorite, Habanero Sea Salt, the caramel that hurts so good!

Tops for Shoes SHOES
(Map p87; www.topsforshoes.com; 27 N Lexington Ave; ⊙10am-6pm Mon-Sat, 1-5pm Sun) This may look like a run-of-the-mill, old-school shoe store, but venture inside – it's enormous, with an eye-catching assortment of hiking boots and hip footwear.

Malaprop's Bookstore & Cafe BOOKS
(Map p87; ✑828-254-6734; www.malaprops.com; 55 Haywood St; ⊙9am-9pm Mon-Sat, to 7pm Sun; ☏) Downtown's best-loved new bookstore is cherished locally for its expert staff, who maintain a carefully curated selection of regional fiction and nonfiction. The cappuccino and wi-fi are very welcome too.

ⓘ Information

Asheville's main **visitor center** (Map p87; ✑828-258-6129; www.exploreasheville.com; 36 Montford Ave; ⊙8:30am-5:30pm Mon-Fri, 9am-5pm Sat & Sun), alongside I-240 exit 4C, sells Biltmore Estate admission tickets at a $10 discount. Downtown holds a satellite **visitor pavilion** (Map p87; ✑828-258-6129; 80 Court Pl; ⊙9am-5pm), with restrooms, beside Pack Sq Park.

ⓘ Getting There & Away

Asheville Regional Airport (AVL; ✑828-684-2226; www.flyavl.com; 61 Terminal Dr, Fletcher), 16 miles south of Asheville, is served by a handful of nonstop flights, with destinations including Atlanta, Charlotte, Chicago and New York.
Greyhound (Map p89; ✑828-253-8451; www.greyhound.com; 2 Tunnel Rd) is 1 mile northeast of downtown.

WESTERN NORTH CAROLINA

North Carolina's westernmost tip is blanketed in parkland and sprinkled with tiny mountain towns. The region is rich in Native American history. A large proportion of its Cherokee population was forced off their lands during the 1830s – by their erstwhile ally, Andrew Jackson – and marched to Oklahoma on the Trail of Tears, but many managed to hide in the remote mountains.

Their descendants, now known as the Eastern Band of Cherokee Indians, live on the 56,000-acre Qualla Boundary territory, on the southern edge of Great Smoky Mountains National Park (p100).

Rolling across western North Carolina into the mountainous High Country, the contiguous Pisgah and Nantahala National Forests hold more than a million acres of dense hardwood trees and windswept mountain balds, as well as some of the country's best white-water rapids – and sections of the Appalachian Trail.

Cherokee
✑828 / POP 2136

To most visitors, Cherokee is a typical and rather unlovely gateway town, guarding the southern approaches to Great Smoky Mountains National Park, and lined with tacky souvenir shops and fast-food joints, which culminate in the out-of-place spectacle of Harrah's Cherokee Casino. To the Eastern Band of Cherokee Indians, however, this is the headquarters of the Qualla Boundary, an area of tribal-owned land that is not officially a reservation. As such, it holds a major historical museum – the Museum of the Cherokee Indian, p51 – and a fine traditional crafts gallery (p96).

🛏 Sleeping & Eating

Harrah's Cherokee Hotel CASINO HOTEL $$
(Map p102; ✑828-497-7777; www.caesars.com/harrahs-cherokee; 777 Casino Dr; r from $179; ✷☏☲) While it's hardly rural or rustic, this enormous and ever-expanding casino resort holds more than 1000 high-quality hotel rooms, which are larger and more comfortable than anything else you'll find in Cherokee. It also offers indoor and outdoor pools, a spa, and a dozen restaurants.

Sassy Sunflowers BAKERY $
(Map p102; ✑828-497-2539; www.facebook.com/sassysunflowers; 1655 Acquoni Rd; sandwiches & salads $8-10; ⊙9am-4pm Mon-Fri; ☏✐) For a wholesome lunch or breakfast, stop to eat a sandwich and salad at the outdoor tables of this cheery roadside bakery-cafe. As well as turkey, chicken and prime rib, the menu includes vegetarian choices such as their signature Sunflower Salad, featuring goat's cheese, apple, cranberries and sunflower seeds.

It's south of the river, immediately outside Great Smoky Mountains National Park.

GATLINBURG, TENNESSEE

Wildly kitschy and family-friendly Gatlinburg hunkers at the entrance to Great Smoky Mountains National Park, waiting to stun hikers with the scent of fudge, cotton candy and pancakes, and with various odd museums and campy attractions. Boisterous new tasting rooms are drawing thirsty adult crowds to a slew of moonshine distilleries along Parkway, the main drag through town that rolls right into the national park. It's a wild ride of all that's good and bad about the USA at the same time, wrapped up in a gaudy explosion of magic shows and whiskey. For the most part, the town emerged from the devastating 2016 wildfires largely unscathed, but memories of the conflagration linger.

For lofty views of the Smokies, hop aboard one of the many ski lifts and gondolas whisking visitors up to gorgeous mountain summits. If you're short on time, settle into the **Gatlinburg Sky Lift** (Map p102; ☏ 865-436-4307; www.gatlinburgskylift.com; 765 Parkway; adult/child $16/13; ⊙ 9am-11pm Jun-Aug, hr vary rest of year). For a tree canopy walk, outdoor dining and an exhibit about the 2016 fires, spend some time at the new **Anakeesta** (Map p102; ☏ 865-325-2400; www.anakeesta.com; 576 Parkway; adult/child under 12yr $20/16; ⊙ generally 10am-7pm Sun-Thu, to 8pm Fri & Sat; P ♿). Un-aged corn whiskey, better known as moonshine, is a regional specialty. Two distilleries serving samples to happy crowds are **Ole Smoky Moonshine Holler** (Map p102; ☏ 865-436-6995; www.olesmoky.com; 903 Parkway; tasting $5; ⊙ 10am-10pm) and nearby **Sugarlands Distilling Co** (Map p102; ☏ 865-325-1355; www.sugarlands.com; 805 Parkway; tasting $5; ⊙ 10am-10:30pm Mon-Sat, noon-6:30pm Sun). Hearty breakfasts are the specialty at **Crockett's Breakfast Camp** (Map p102; ☏ 865-325-1403; www.crockettsbreakfastcamp.com; 1103 Parkway; mains $7-15; ⊙ 7am-1pm), a faux hunting lodge named for a local frontiersman.

🍷 Drinking & Entertainment

Qualla Java Cafe COFFEE
(Map p102; ☏ 828-497-2882; www.quallajava.com; 938 Tsalagi Rd; ⊙ 7am-5pm Mon-Fri, from 8am Sat, from 9am Sun; 🛜) This welcoming little Cherokee-owned coffee bar, conspicuous for its towering pointed roof alongside the highway, is a good place to kick off the day.

Harrah's Cherokee Casino CASINO
(Map p102; ☏ 828-497-7777; www.caesars.com/harrahs-cherokee; 777 Casino Dr; ⊙ 24hr; 🛜) As well as all the usual casino games, this high-rise complex holds a towering hotel block (p95), two swimming pools, a spa and restaurants of all kinds. There's also an impressive water-and-video display in the lobby.

🛍 Shopping

Qualla Arts & Crafts Mutual ARTS & CRAFTS
(Map p102; ☏ 828-497-3103; www.quallaartsandcrafts.com; 645 Tsali Blvd/Hwy 441, cnr Drama Rd; ⊙ 9am-4:30pm, closed Sun Jan & Feb) To pick up authentic Cherokee craftwork, including basketry, stone carving and ceramics, head to this large cooperative gallery.

ℹ Getting There & Away

Cherokee's nearest airport is Asheville Regional Airport (p95), 55 miles east.

Brevard

☏ 828 / POP 7822

One of those charming little mountain towns that set travelers daydreaming of putting down roots, Brevard is also a top destination for mountain bikers, with numerous trails ripping through the nearby Dupont State Forest and Pisgah National Forest. Brevard is the seat of the ominous-sounding Transylvania County, which more appealingly styles itself as 'Land of Waterfalls.' Visitors flock year-round to enjoy the surrounding scenery.

The town is also the home of the prestigious Brevard Music Center, a summer school for music students that also stages the Brevard Music Festival.

🏃 Activities

Brevard makes an ideal base for bikers and hikers, who come to explore the myriad trails, swimming holes and waterfalls hidden away in the slopes of the Pisgah Ranger District of Pisgah National Forest.

Hub MOUNTAIN BIKING
(☏ 828-884-8670; www.thehubpisgah.com; 11 Mama's Place, Pisgah Forest; bike rental per day from $40; ⊙ 10am-6pm Mon-Fri, from 9am Sat, 10am-5pm Sun) Even if you're traveling with all the

right gear and equipment, and don't need to rent from the Hub's extensive array of bikes, be sure to call in at this excellent outfitters for advice and updates on the countless mountain and forest trails nearby.

This being North Carolina, it also incorporates its own brewpub, the Pisgah Tavern.

🎉 Festivals & Events

Brevard Music Festival MUSIC
(☎828-862-2100; www.brevardmusic.org; Brevard Music Center, 349 Andante Lane; ⊙ Jun–mid-Aug) The prestigious Brevard Music Center runs this summer-long festival, staging more than 80 concerts, ranging from classical and opera to bluegrass and movie music, in various venues around town.

🛏️ Sleeping & Eating

Brevard offers accommodations to suit all budgets, including campgrounds in the adjoining public lands.

Davidson River Campground CAMPGROUND $
(☎828-862-5960; www.recreation.gov; 1 Davidson River Circle, Pisgah Forest; tent sites $22-44) At the southern edge of the most spectacular stretch of Pisgah National Forest, 5 miles north of downtown Brevard, this riverside campground – tubing optional! – is better suited to tenters than RVs. The facilities are relatively basic, but the wooded setting is idyllic. Silence is requested, and insisted on, from 10pm to 7am.

Hike trails of all levels or just sling a hammock between the trees.

Sunset Motel MOTEL $
(☎828-884-9106; http://thesunsetmotel.com; 523 S Broad St; r from $99; 🅿🛜) They don't make 'em like the Sunset Motel anymore, so if you've a penchant for vintage motor lodges, and you don't mind every last fixture and fitting looking like it came straight from the 1950s, you won't want to miss it. Choose from cabins, apartments and standard motel rooms, and don't worry – they've got wi-fi and 21st-century TVs too.

Red House Inn B&B $$
(☎828-884-9349; www.brevardbedandbreakfast. com; 266 W Probart St; r from $160; 🅿🛜) Built as a general store in 1851, the Red House went through various incarnations before becoming a B&B. Set in stately repose five minutes' walk from downtown, it offers superbly quiet, tastefully furnished en suite rooms, plus full cooked breakfasts.

The owners also rent out fully equipped vacation homes nearby.

Falls Landing SEAFOOD $$
(☎828-884-2835; www.thefallslanding.com; 18 E Main St; dinner mains $15-28; ⊙11:30am-3pm Mon, 11:30am-3pm & 5-9pm Tue-Sat) Brevard's favorite fine-dining restaurant works wonders with fish – the owner moved here from the Virgin Islands, and is as happy serving oysters or crab cakes as pan-frying fresh NC trout – but there's plenty more besides, including lamb chops and rib-eye.

Burgers ($9) stay on the menu all day, joined by sandwiches at lunchtime.

🍷 Drinking & Nightlife

Brevard Brewing Co MICROBREWERY
(☎828-885-2101; www.brevard-brewing.com; 63 E Main St; ⊙2-11pm Mon-Thu, noon-midnight Fri & Sat, 2-10pm Sun; 🛜) Though it's right in the heart of town, this small local brewery (pints from $3.50) always seems to have a peaceful, welcoming vibe. It specializes in German lagers and pilsners, but also makes an American IPA, as well as seasonal variations including a coriander ale in fall. There's no food.

ℹ️ Getting There & Away

In the absence of public transportation, you'll almost certainly have to drive to Brevard. Ideally, make your way here on the Blue Ridge Parkway, heading south on Hwy 276 from Mile 412.

Pisgah National Forest

Pisgah National Forest extends across huge swathes of North Carolina's mountains, curling around Asheville in a convoluted but not quite joined-up circle. To the northeast it includes most of the Blue Ridge Parkway between Blowing Rock and Asheville, extending almost to the summit of Mt Mitchell, while to the north it stretches via Hot Springs to the edge of the Smokies.

The section of the forest southwest of Asheville, known as the Pisgah Ranger District and incorporating parts of the original Biltmore Estate (p49), offers wonderful recreational opportunities. It's best approached by leaving the Blue Ridge Parkway at Mile 412. Immediately north of here looms the forested bulk of Cold Mountain, immortalized in Charles Frazier's 1997 book and the subsequent movie. Head south on Hwy 276, and en route to the delightful country town of Brevard, you'll pass several potential stop-offs as well as a helpful ranger station.

For information and advice on the Pisgah Ranger District, call in at either the **ranger station** (☏ 828-877-3265; www.cfaia.org; 1600 Pisgah Hwy/Hwy 276; ⏰ 9am-5pm mid-Apr–mid-Nov, 8:30am-4:30pm mid-Nov–mid-Apr) or Brevard's Hub (p97), which also rents out bikes and outdoor equipment.

All three districts of Pisgah National Forest are readily accessible from, and connected by, the Blue Ridge Parkway.

Sliding Rock Recreation Area   WATERFALL
(☏ 828-885-7625; www.fs.usda.gov; Pisgah Hwy/Hwy 276; $2; ⏰ staffed 9am-6pm late May–early Sep; P) For a totally exhilarating stop on a journey along the Blue Ridge Parkway, stop off and strip down at Sliding Rock, 7 miles off the parkway. Propelled down this natural 60ft slide of smooth, gently sloping granite by 11,000 gallons of cool stream water per minute, bathers splash into a pool that's up to 8ft deep; swimming skills are essential. If possible, time your visit to avoid the noon-to-4pm crowds.

Lifeguards are present daily in summer, on weekends in fall. When they're not, changing rooms and restrooms are closed, and you should be very wary of entering the water.

Cradle of Forestry in America   NATURE CENTER
(☏ 828-877-3130; www.cradleofforestry.com; 11250 Pisgah Hwy/Hwy 276; adult/child under 13yr $6/3; ⏰ 9am-5pm early Apr–mid-Nov; P) The spot where scientific forestry management was first attempted in the US, financed by George Vanderbilt back in 1895, is now a showcase for the Forest Service. Amid the original log cabins, 4 miles off Blue Ridge Parkway, a visitor center holds interactive exhibits targeted at children, including a scary simulation of a helicopter flying over a forest fire. Paved trails lead through the woods themselves.

Bryson City

☏ 828 / POP 1452
This tiny, charming mountain town straddling the Tuckasegee River is not only a cute little base for exploring Great Smoky Mountains National Park (p100), but an adventure destination in its own right. Handily poised for Nantahala National Forest, it's a great spot for water sports such as rafting and kayaking. You might remember it from Cormac McCarthy's 1979 novel, *Suttree* – the title character winds up here after wandering over the mountains from Gatlinburg.

Home to a smattering of good restaurants and breweries, Bryson City is also the starting point for the Great Smoky Mountains Railroad, which leaves from a historic depot downtown.

🏃 Activities

Class II and III white-water rafting on the Nantahala River, 12 miles west of Bryson City, draws more than 200,000 paddlers per year, while the Tuckasegee in town is a popular spot for fishing, paddleboarding and kayaking. The Deep Creek Recreation Area, 1.7 miles north of downtown, offers tubing and waterfalls.

Bryson City Bicycles   CYCLING
(Map p102; ☏ 828-488-1988; www.brysoncitybicycles.com; 157 Everett St; mountain-bike rentals per 24hr from $40; ⏰ 10am-6pm Tue-Sat) Quite apart from meeting all possible bike needs, including equipment sales, repairs and rentals, this friendly bike shop is worth its weight in saddlebags for the expert and freely given advice on local biking trail networks.

Road to Nowhere   HIKING
(Map p102; Lakeview Dr;) The so-called Road to Nowhere – officially, Lakeview Dr – leads northwest of Bryson City towards Great Smoky Mountains National Park (p100). It was intended as a scenic drive, but only 6 miles were completed. For a quirky hike, park where the road ends, then keep on walking through the 1200ft tunnel beyond; alternative trails loop back in either 2.2 or 3.2 miles.

👣 Tours

Great Smoky Mountains Railroad   RAIL
(Map p102; ☏ 800-872-4681; www.gsmr.com; 226 Everett St; Nantahala Gorge trip adult/child 2-12yr from $58/34; ⏰ schedules vary;) These scenic train excursions, lasting around four hours, follow two alternate routes – either east along the Tuckasegee River to Dills-

boro, or southwest to the spectacular Nantahala Gorge. Up to four trains run daily on peak summer and fall weekends.

🛏 Sleeping & Eating

★ Everett Hotel   BOUTIQUE HOTEL $$
(Map p102; 📞828-488-1976; www.theeveretthotel.com; 24 Everett St; r from $199; 🅿 🛜) This nine-room boutique hotel occupies a century-old building that once housed western North Carolina's first bank. Beautiful pinewood hallways lead to rooms awash in a mineral-grey palette, with plantation shutters and wonderful dark-stained pinewood ceilings. A fire pit warms the scenic rooftop terrace. Rates include an à la carte breakfast in the excellent house bistro.

Fryemont Inn   INN $$
(Map p102; 📞828-488-2159; www.fryemontinn.com; 245 Fryemont St; lodge/ste/cabin from $165/205/260; ⊙mid-Apr–late Nov; 🅿 🛜 🏊) The views of the Smokies from this lofty bark-covered mountain lodge are unbeatable. Rooms lack TVs and air-con, but rates include breakfast and dinner in the on-site public restaurant (open 8am to 10am and 6pm to 8pm), which serves trout, steak and lamb. The lodge itself closes in winter, as does its restaurant, but the cottage and balcony suites – the only areas with wi-fi reception – remain open.

For nonguests, breakfast in the restaurant costs $10 to $12, while dinner mains are $20 to $31.

Bistro at the Everett Hotel   BISTRO $$
(Map p102; 📞828-488-1934; www.theeveretthotel.com; 16 Everett St; mains $18-35; ⊙4:30-9pm Mon-Fri, 8:30am-3pm & 4:30-9pm Sat & Sun; 🛜) Big windows frame this classy downtown bar-restaurant, where the emphasis is on organic local ingredients, and there are local craft beers on tap. Typical dinner mains include meatloaf, mountain trout and scallops on goat's-cheese grits, while the weekend brunch menu features eggs Benedict and huevos rancheros.

🍸 Drinking & Nightlife

Nantahala Brewing Company   MICROBREWERY
(Map p102; 📞828-488-2337; www.nantahalabrewing.com; 61 Depot St; ⊙noon-11pm Sun-Thu, to midnight Fri & Sat May-Aug, reduced hr Sep-Apr; 🛜) In a massive repurposed WWII military Quonset hut, this Bryson City brewery (pints from $5) counts well over 30 taps in its main taproom. Standouts include the Dirty Girl Blonde Ale, Noon Day IPA, and assorted experimental versions using different hops or production methods.

ℹ Getting There & Away
Bryson City is 10 miles west of Cherokee. The closest airport is Asheville Regional Airport (p95), 70 miles east of town.

Nantahala National Forest
The largest of North Carolina's four national forests, Nantahala National Forest covers more than half a million acres of the state's westernmost portion, extending south from Great Smoky Mountains National Park all the way to the South Carolina and Georgia state lines.

The name Nantahala means 'Land of the Noonday Sun' in Cherokee, because only when the sun is at its highest can it penetrate all the way to the floor of the Nantahala Gorge. The gorge itself is in the forest's Nantahala Ranger District, which also holds the tallest waterfall east of the Mississippi. Very close to South Carolina, 26 miles southwest of Brevard, Whitewater Falls can be reached via a steep 1-mile hike from NC 281.

The Tsali Recreation Area is 15 miles west of Bryson City; follow Hwy 74 for 9.6 miles, turn right onto NC 28, and then turn right again onto Tsali Rd (SR 1286) after another 3.4 miles. Follow signs to trailheads and the campground.

Tsali Recreation Area   FOREST
(📞828-479-6431; www.fs.usda.gov; Tsali Rd; ⊙24hr; 🅿) FREE The Tsali Recreation Area has been famed among mountain bikers for so long that local riders rather take it for granted. For out-of-state visitors, though, it offers a great combination of challenging but not overly technical trails, spectacular lake-and-mountain views, and convenient access. All of the four main trails are categorized as moderate, incorporating waterfront stretches beside Fontana Lake plus significant climbs.

The four trails are divided into two groups – the Mouse Branch and Thompson Loops, and the longer Left and Right Loops – each of which is reserved for bikers and horse riders on alternate days. The Left Loop is the toughest trail, with its steep ascents and narrow ledges, while novice

Nantahala Outdoor Center

riders can opt for a short 5-mile ride by tackling only a segment of the less demanding Right Loop. There are restrooms, showers and bike-washing facilities at the parking lot.

Nantahala Outdoor Center RAFTING
(NOC; ☏ 828-366-7502, 828-785-5082; www.noc.com; 13077 Hwy 19 W; duckie rental per day $35, guided trips $50-200; ⊙8am-8pm Jun & Jul, reduced hr Aug-May) This huge and highly recommended outfitter specializes in wet 'n' wild rafting trips down the Nantahala River. Their 500-acre site, located 14 miles southwest of Bryson City, also offers ziplining and mountain biking, and even has its own lodge, a hostel, a mostly year-round restaurant and a seasonal BBQ and beer joint (open from May to October).

The Appalachian Trail rolls across the property too.

Tsali Campground CAMPGROUND $
(☏828-479-6431; www.fs.usda.gov; Tsali Rd; tent sites $15; ⊙Apr-Oct; P) This forest-service campground holds around 40 tent sites, some of which are beside a stream and some that spread across a meadow. It has showers and restrooms, but no electric or water hookups.

GREAT SMOKY MOUNTAINS NATIONAL PARK

ELEV 875FT TO 6643FT

The sun-dappled forests of the **Great Smoky Mountains** (www.nps.gov/grsm) **FREE** are a four-season wonderland. Rich blooms of springtime wildflowers come in all colors and sizes, while flame azaleas light up the high-elevation meadows in summer. Autumn brings its own fiery rewards with quilted hues of orange, burgundy and saffron blanketing the mountain slopes. In winter, snow-covered fields and ice-fringed cascades transform the Smokies into a serene, cold-weather retreat.

The Smokies are part of the vast Appalachian chain, among the oldest mountains on the planet. Formed more than 200 million years ago, these ancient peaks were once much higher – perhaps as high as the Himalayas – but have been worn down by the ages. You can contemplate that remote past while huffing your way up to the top of a 6000ft peak overlooking the seemingly endless expanse of undulating ridges that stretch off into the distance.

History holds tight here too. In small mountain communities around the Smokies, early settlers built log cabins, one-room schoolhouses, stream-fed gristmills and single-steeple churches amid the fertile forest valleys. The park has preserved many of these vestiges of the past, which make up one of the largest collections of log structures in the nation.

⊙ Sights & Activities

The Smokies are packed with clifftop viewpoints, picturesque drives and forested trails that wind past boulder-filled streams to thundering cascades. Early settlers left their mark in the fertile mountain valleys, and you can peer into the past by exploring the park's many old log cabins, schoolhouses and churches.

Cades Cove and the northern part of the park (Tennessee) generally draw more visitors than Cataloochee and the southern half (North Carolina). Dividing the two is the Newfound Gap Rd, which has a little of everything – views, hikes, historic buildings and even occasional wildlife viewing.

⊙ Newfound Gap Road

Historic attractions and gorgeous scenery dot this 33-mile mountain road, which stretches north from Cherokee, NC, to Gatlinburg, TN. Stunning panoramas await at Newfound Gap and atop Clingmans Dome, while trailheads to some of the park's best hiking trails lie along this road.

Sights and activities listed below begin at the Oconaluftee Visitor Center in North Carolina and end near the park's border at Gatlinburg, TN.

Oconaluftee
Visitor Center   TOURIST INFORMATION

(☑828-497-1904; www.nps.gov/grsm; 1194 Newfound Gap Rd, North Cherokee, NC; ⊙8am-7pm Jun-Aug, to 6pm Apr, May, Sep & Oct, to 4:30pm Nov-Mar; 🐾) 🅿 At the park's southern entrance, near Cherokee, NC, this is the park's only LEED-certified visitor center. Its exhibits trace the cultural history of the region and provide fascinating insight into the indigenous people and the settlers who lived here before the park's establishment.

The shop is an excellent resource, with books, detailed maps, walking sticks, clothing items, souvenirs and activities for kids (puzzles, mini binoculars, junior ranger books). There's free wi-fi – useful for booking campsites if you show up to the park without reservations.

Mountain Farm Museum   MUSEUM

(www.nps.gov/grsm; Newfound Gap Rd, Cherokee; ⊙9am-5pm mid-Mar–mid-Nov & Thanksgiving weekend) Adjacent to the Oconaluftee Visitor Center, this excellent collection of historic buildings evokes life on a typical farmstead of the late 19th century. Together these structures paint a poignant picture of the mountain people who once eked out their sustenance from this rugged and isolated wilderness.

The wooden buildings are authentic, but were moved here from other parts of the national park in the 1950s. One of the first buildings you come to is the meat house, where a mountain farm's most valuable commodity (usually pork) was butchered, dried and smoked or salted for preservation.

Other structures are dedicated to apples (used for apple sauce, apple butter, cider, vinegar, apple pies and for eating raw), sorghum (used to make molasses) and corn (the most important crop on mountain farms, used for cornmeal and fresh corn, while its shucks were stuffed into mattresses and woven into chair seats, dolls, rugs and brooms). In the summer you can also see live hogs and chickens – a requisite stop for families with small children. A terrific time to visit is in mid-September for the **Mountain Life Festival**.

Oconaluftee River Trail   HIKING

(🐾) This flat, peaceful trail follows along the banks of the pretty Oconaluftee River. Go around dawn or dusk and you may see elk grazing in the fields. The 3-mile, round-trip walk begins just outside the Oconaluftee Visitor Center.

This is one of only two trails in the park that allows dogs, as long as they're on a leash (the other dog-friendly path is the Gatlinburg Trail; p105). You can also ride a bike along the trail.

Mingus Mill   HISTORIC BUILDING

(Mingus Creek Trail, off Newfound Gap Rd, Cherokee; ⊙9am-5pm mid-Mar–mid-Nov & Thanksgiving weekend) FREE One of the park's most picturesque 19th-century buildings, the Mingus Mill is a turbine-powered mill that still grinds wheat and corn much as it has since its opening back in 1886. You're welcome to explore the multistory structure, checking out its clever engineering mechanisms and walking the length of its 200ft-long flume that brings water from a stream to the mill's turbine. It's located about a

Great Smoky Mountains

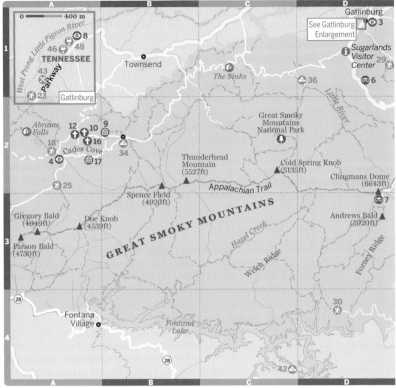

mile north of the Oconaluftee Visitor Center (and 4 miles north of Cherokee).

There's usually a park employee on site who can share details on how the whole operation works. There's also a small stand near the entrance where you can purchase ground cornmeal (not milled on site, but still made the old-fashioned way).

Instagram filters unnecessary for this photogenic timber structure!

Smokemont
Riding Stables   HORSEBACK RIDING
(☏828-497-2373; www.smokemontridingstable.com; 135 Smokemont Riding Stable Rd; 1/4hr ride $35/140, wagon ride $15; ⊙9am-5pm mid-Mar–Oct) Offers one- and four-hour horseback rides as well as waterfall and wagon rides.

Kephart Prong Trail   HIKING
(off Newfound Gap Rd) This moderate 4.2-mile (round trip) hike takes you through thick forest to the ruins of an old Civilian Conservation Corps camp built during the Great Depression. It's located about 0.2 miles from the trailhead. Further along, you'll have some fine views of the churning Kephart Prong and make several scenic crossings of the fern-dappled river on log bridges.

The trail ends near the Kephart Shelter, a popular backcountry site for backpackers. From here a left turn along the Sweat Heifer Creek trail goes 3.7 miles uphill to intersect with the Appalachian Trail.

The trailhead is located along the park's main north–south road, about 7 miles north of the Oconaluftee Visitor Center.

Newfound Gap   VIEWPOINT
(Newfound Gap Rd) The lowest drivable pass through the Smoky Mountains is located here, at 5046ft. After the pass was discovered in 1872, a new road followed suit, eventually becoming today's Newfound Gap

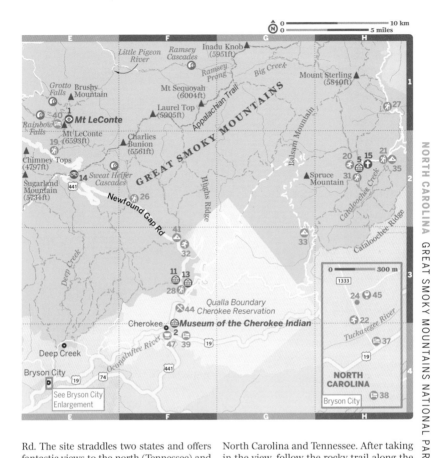

Rd. The site straddles two states and offers fantastic views to the north (Tennessee) and south (North Carolina). The rocky platform is where you'll find the **Rockefeller Memorial**. It was on this spot on September 2, 1940 that President Franklin Roosevelt formally dedicated the park.

The Appalachian Trail travels right across Newfound Gap (you may see a few hungry hikers trying to hitch a ride up to Gatlinburg for a soft bed and a warm meal). This is also the starting point for the hike to Charlies Bunion (p103). Newfound Gap is around 13 miles south of the Sugarlands Visitor Center (p105).

Charlies Bunion   HIKING
(Newfound Gap, Newfound Gap Rd) This oddly named outcropping along the Appalachian Trail offers staggering views. The popular 8-mile (round-trip) trail starts near the Rockefeller Memorial, which straddles North Carolina and Tennessee. After taking in the view, follow the rocky trail along the ridgeline, ascending 1000ft over the first 2.5 miles, then making a gentle descent before another brief uphill push to Charlies Bunion.

You'll arrive at the craggy promontory with its dazzling panorama sweeping from Mt LeConte eastward to the the jagged peaks of the Sawteeth Range. It's a great spot for a picnic, though be careful where you step, as some hikers have fallen to their deaths while scrambling around on the rock face.

The trailhead is at Newfound Gap, on the road of the same name, around 13 miles south of the Sugarlands Visitor Center.

Clingmans Dome   VIEWPOINT
(off Clingmans Dome Rd) 'On top of Old Smoky' is Clingmans Dome (elevation 6643ft), the park's highest peak. At the summit, a steep,

Great Smoky Mountains

half-mile paved trail leads to an observation tower offering a 360-degree view of the Smokies and beyond. It can be cold and foggy up here, even when the sun is shining in Sugarlands, so bring a jacket. The tower resembles something of a flying saucer, with a gently curving ramp leading up to the top.

Panels around the viewing platform indicate names of the surrounding peaks and distant places of interest.

As one of the must-see sights in the park, Clingmans Dome gets crowded, especially in the summer. Note that the 7-mile access road to Newfound Gap Rd is closed to vehicles from December through March. The viewpoint is open year-round, however, for those willing to hike in – take care on the trails, which can be icy even in March or April.

Alum Cave Bluffs　　　　HIKING
(off Newfound Gap Rd) The well-loved, 4.6-mile round-trip Alum Cave Bluffs hike provides a representative sampling of the park's diverse pleasures. Some rate this satisfying hike, which passes through old-growth forest and follows a series of streams as it winds its way up the southern slope of Mt LeConte, to be the finest in the park.

The pleasures of the hike must be earned, however; it's a steady climb to the bluffs.

Highlights include **Arch Rock**, where handcrafted stone steps ascend steeply through the portal of an impressive stone arch that looks like something Frodo was compelled to climb. Beyond this interesting formation, the trail crosses the Styx Branch and begins a steep ascent. The forest gives way to open sky at the next point of interest, a large heath bald where mountain laurel and blueberry bushes grow in a dense mass. After some huffing and puffing, you'll be repaid for your efforts at a scenic vista called Inspiration Point. From here, it's a short climb to Alum Cave Bluffs. As it turns out, the name is a misnomer. Waiting for you is not a cave, but rather a rock overhang. Moreover, the rocks contain not alum, but sulfur and rare minerals, some not known to occur elsewhere. If you're game for more delightful punishment, you can continue on from Alum Cave Bluffs to the summit of Mt LeConte, 2.7 miles up the trail. Access the trailhead from Newfound Gap Rd.

★ Mt LeConte   MOUNTAIN
Mt LeConte (6593ft) is the park's third-highest peak and one of its most familiar sights, visible from practically every viewpoint. The only way to get to the top is on foot. It is accessible on five trails, which range from 5 to 8.9 miles in length. Near the summit, LeConte Lodge (p111) is the park's only non-camping lodging, but you better book ahead.

Reaching the summit (located 0.2 miles above the lodge) is a challenging goal, but it's well worth the effort. Aside from great views, you can stop in the office and lounge at LeConte Lodge to check out photos of cabin life dating back to the 1930s. A small shop sells T-shirts, socks, rain ponchos and other essentials, while you can pick up a sack lunch ($11), cookies ($1) or drink bottomless cups of coffee, hot chocolate or lemonade (all $4) at the restaurant.

Carlos C Campbell Overlook   VIEWPOINT
(Newfound Gap Rd) This scenic overlook provides a sweeping view of the various types of forests covering the slopes to the east. You'll see spruce-fir forest at the top, northern hardwood below, hemlock forest nestled in the valley and, just to the north, cove hardwood forest. You can also spy pine-oak forest and a small heath bald. A signpost helps show where to look to see the different forest features.

The scene is at its most dramatic in autumn, when golds, reds and oranges blaze across the mountain.

The overlook is located about 2.5 miles south of the Sugarlands Visitor Center. Look for the small parking area to the left as you're driving south.

Sugarlands Visitor Center   TOURIST INFORMATION
(☏ 865-436-1291; www.nps.gov/grsm; 107 Park Headquarters Rd; ◷ 8am-7:30pm Jun-Aug, hr vary Sep-May; ☎) At the park's northern entrance near Gatlinburg, the Sugarlands Visitor Center has helpful park rangers on hand to advise on hiking trails and other activities. Out the back, you'll find displays on native plants and animals that you may later spot in the park. It's also worth attending a free screening of a 20-minute film on the park.

There's a good shop and bookstore here.

Gatlinburg Trail   HIKING
(River Rd, off Hwy 441 S; 🚴🐾) Although this 2-mile, one-way trail is completely within the national park, its northern trailhead borders downtown Gatlinburg, enticing folks into the woods and away from the Ripley's museums and pancake houses. Pet and bike friendly, the easy trail parallels the West Prong of the Little Pigeon River and passes the ruins of old homesteads before ending at the Sugarlands Visitor Center.

Rainbow Falls   HIKING
(off Cherokee Orchard Rd) Seeing these falls takes a bit of dedication (and lung power) – you must ascend 1600ft in a scant 2.7 miles. But oh, is it worth it. A long slog is finally rewarded by the sight of the misty Rainbow Falls, one of the park's prettiest and most delicate waterfalls.

Rivulets of crystalline water spill over an 80ft bluff and then flow through a mossy boulder field in a succession of gentle cascades.

The entire trail is about 5.4 miles in length and takes about four hours (round trip) to hike. The trailhead is off Roaring Fork Motor Nature Trail. Note that trail maintenance is underway, likely through 2019, and from Monday to Thursday the trail will be closed.

◉ Cades Cove

There's something about the morning light in Cades Cove, Tennessee. With mountain-flanked meadows aglow under the golden rays, and deer, turkeys and black bears cavorting in the shimmering grasses, the scene is memorably enchanting. Unfortunately, with two million visitors exploring this valley every year, immersing yourself in that magic can be a challenge, particularly in

CADES COVE: NEED TO KNOW

➡ Cades Cove Loop Rd is open to motor vehicles from sunrise to sunset.

➡ The road is closed to vehicle traffic until 10am on Wednesday and Saturday between early May and late September. This a great time for cyclists and pedestrians to travel the loop.

➡ The 11-mile loop road is one way. Sparks Lane and Hyatt Lane offer shortcuts if you don't want to drive the full 11 miles.

➡ Use the roadside pullouts if you want to take a long look at the scenery or wildlife. There are also parking spaces at the numbered stops.

➡ There is no overnight parking in the picnic area. If you plan to camp in the nearby backcountry, park in the lot beside the campground store (p111).

➡ The busiest times to visit are summer and the fall foliage season, as well as weekends year-round.

➡ There are restrooms at the visitor center (p111), beside the campground store, at the campground and in the picnic area. You'll find pit toilets at the Abrams Falls trailhead parking lot.

➡ You can buy firewood and ice cream at the campground store.

summer and fall when bumper-to-bumper traffic jams the 11-mile loop road. The one-way road encircles land used as a hunting ground by the Cherokee before English, Scots-Irish and German settlers arrived in the 1820s. These determined newcomers built cabins and churches while clearing the valley's trees for farmland. Mills, forges and blacksmith shops soon followed, creating a thriving community. Today the creaky cabins, mossy spring houses, weathered barns and tidy cemeteries whisper the stories of the families who made this place their home. You'll hear them best if you arrive before 9am.

The sights and activities below are listed in the order in which they appear on the loop road.

John Oliver Place   HISTORIC BUILDING
(Cades Cove Loop Rd; P) Built in the early 1820s, this rustic log cabin is the oldest in Cades Cove. Check out the stone chimney, made with mud mortar. The home was built by one of the cove's earliest settlers and remained in the family until the park was founded more than 100 years later.

Primitive Baptist Church   CHURCH
(Cades Cove Loop Rd; P) One of three rural churches that remain standing in Cades Cove, the 1887 Primitive Baptist Church is flanked by an atmospheric cemetery. Look out for the grave of Russell Gregory, 'mur-

dered by North Carolina rebels' during the Civil War for being a Union sympathizer.

Methodist Church   CHURCH
(Cades Cove Loop Rd; P) Cades Cove's 1902 Methodist Church has a small but picturesque white steeple and includes gravestones on its lawn. It was built by blacksmith and carpenter JD McCampbell in 115 days for $115.

Note the two entrance/exit doors, which normally indicates that the church separated men and woman within the congregation, but that wasn't the case with the Methodist Church. It had simply borrowed building plans from a church that did separate its congregation, so two doors were built.

Missionary Baptist Church   CHURCH
(Cades Cove Loop Rd) The Missionary Baptist Church was formed in 1839 by former Primitive Baptist Church members who were kicked out for advocating missionary work. The building itself dates to 1915.

Abrams Falls   HIKING
(Cades Cove Loop Rd) The 5-mile round-trip hike to Abrams Falls is the most popular walk in Cades Cove, and for good reason. After following the boisterous Abrams Creek and its many tributaries, you will arrive at an enormously appealing waterfall that spills into one of the park's largest natural pools.

The beauty of this place is certainly no secret, and unless it's a gray and rainy day, you can expect to share the experience with scores of others. Try to arrive by 9am, if not earlier, to beat the crowds.

You'll find the turnoff for the trailhead 5 miles from the beginning of Cades Cove Loop Rd, just prior to the Cable Mill area. Be careful around the mossy rocks at the bottom of the falls – they're highly slippery and there have been numerous accidents in recent years.

Cable Mill Historic Area   HISTORIC SITE

(Cades Cove Loop Rd; P) To get bread on the table, early residents of Cades Cove first had to mill their grains and corn. Above all other staples, corn was the most important. Every meal included food made from cornmeal, including corn bread, mush, hoecakes and spoon bread. Built in the early 1870s by John Cable, Cable Mill was once one of four or five water-powered gristmills to serve Cades Cove, which reached a peak population of about 700 residents by 1900.

Powered by Mill Creek, the waters of which were routed into the mill via a 235ft-long flume, Cable Mill features a classic overshot waterwheel. The other historic buildings surrounding the mill were brought from other locations in the park to create a living history museum. There's a blacksmith shop, a barn, a smokehouse, a sorghum mill and a homestead, as well as the Cades Cove Visitor Center (p111) and shop – stop by to pick up a bag of corn ground on-site.

Gregory Bald   HIKING

(Forge Creek Rd, off Cades Cove Loop Rd) This 11-mile out-and-back hike on the Gregory Ridge and Gregory Bald Trails follows rough-and-tumble Forge Creek, swings past a campsite nestled in old-growth forest, climbs past oaks and mountain laurel then tops out at a 4949ft-high grassy bald with stunning mountain-and-valley views stretching in almost every direction. In June the summit is ablaze with bright blooms of flame azaleas.

Just past the Cades Cove Visitor Center parking lot, leave the Cades Cove Loop Rd and drive south on Forge Creek Rd for just over 2 miles. The road ends at a small parking area at the trailhead for the 4.9-mile Gregory Ridge Trail. At the end of the Gregory Ridge Trail, pick up the steep Gregory Bald Trail and follow it just over half a mile to the bald.

Tipton Place   HISTORIC BUILDING

(Cades Cove Loop Rd; P) The picturesque Tipton homestead was built by Mexican War veteran 'Colonel Hamp' Tipton in the early 1870s. The grounds include a spacious two-floor cabin, blacksmith and carpentry shops, and a replica cantilever barn.

Cades Cove Trading   CYCLING

(☑ 865-448-9034; www.cadescovetrading.com/bikes; adult per hr $7.50, child under 10yr $4.50; ⊙ 9am-9pm late May-Oct, to 5pm Mar-late May, Nov & last week of Dec, closed rest of the year) Rents cruisers and hybrid bicycles in a building beside the campground store (p111). Opens at 6:30am on Wednesday and Saturday from late May through late September when the loop road is closed to automobile traffic until 10am – and is perfect for cycling!

◉ Cataloochee Valley

Tucked in a far-flung corner of the park, deep in the mountains of western North Carolina, Cataloochee feels untamed. It takes an edge-of-your-seat drive to get here, elk and turkey strut around like they own the place and stories of hermits and wild men give the woods a spooky edge. But it wasn't always so. In 1910 the community – comprising Big Cataloochee and Little Cataloochee – was the largest settlement in the Smokies, with 1251 citizens. Farming, apple production and tourism kept the economy buzzing right up until the late 1920s, when folks heard rumors that the park was moving in. Today historic buildings and lush meadows line Cataloochee Rd in Big Cataloochee Valley, which could double as a safari park with all the wildlife roaming between its 6000ft-high peaks. Over Noland Mountain lies Little Cataloochee Valley, where the sights can only be explored by foot or horseback.

Caldwell House   HISTORIC BUILDING

(Cataloochee Rd; P) With its weatherboarding, interior paneling and shingled gables, as well as its white exterior and jaunty blue trim, this frame house, built in 1906, seems almost of the modern era.

The L-shaped front porch is a pleasant place to soak up the history and the scenery, which includes a stream rippling out front, a photogenic barn and the sound of birds singing in the background.

WILDLIFE WATCHING: ELK

The park service released 25 elk into Cataloochee Valley in 2001. Another 27 were released the following year. Elk had once roamed the southern Appalachian Mountains but overhunting and habitat loss caused their decline and eventual disappearance. The last elk in the region was killed in 1850. Some have migrated from the valley to other parts of the park, but a significant number still graze in the meadows and woods of Cataloochee, particularly along Cataloochee Rd. You'll most likely see them grazing in the early morning and late evening. Stay at least 50yd from the elk. Adult males typically weigh 700lb to 800lb, while females clock in at 500lb. They can reach a height of 5ft. Females with calves could charge you if they feel their offspring is threatened.

Pick up the free *Return of the Elk* brochure at one of the information kiosks along Cataloochee Rd for more details about elk behavior in various seasons. Frisky males sound their loud bugle calls in the fall.

Wild turkeys and white-tail deer also roam the valley, so pack your binoculars and a good camera.

Palmer Chapel   CHURCH
(Cataloochee Rd; P) No, this Methodist church isn't turning its back on Cataloochee Rd. Built in 1898, it faces the old road that once ran through the valley. Circuit-riding preachers visited the chapel one Sunday per month. Today the bright-white church hosts the annual Cataloochee Reunion, when old timers and the descendants of valley families gather to share memories and news. The reunion was held for the 80th time in 2017, and shows no signs of slowing down.

Big Cataloochee Valley   WILDLIFE WATCHING
Early morning and late evening are the best times to look for elk and wild turkey in Big Cataloochee. Two great spots for wildlife watching are the open fields beside Palmer Chapel (p107) and the mountain-flanked meadow behind the Caldwell House (p107) barn. On the way to the latter, you'll find a box of brochures about the local elk population.

Boogerman Loop Hike   HIKING
(Cataloochee Rd) Soaring old-growth trees, lonely stone walls and stories of a shy hermit lend a fairy-tale vibe to this 7.5-mile lasso loop that begins near Cataloochee Campground (p111). The mature trees that mark this hike are here thanks to the hermit, Robert 'Boogerman' Palmer, who did not allow logging on his property. He requested the nickname in elementary school, we hear.

The hike begins with a creekside ramble on the Caldwell Fork Trail, open to hikers and horseback riders. After 0.8 miles the path intersects with the 4.1-mile Boogerman Trail, open only to hikers. From here, you'll climb through a forest wonderland, passing eastern hemlocks, oaks, maples, tulip trees and white pines. The trail rises and falls, passing Palmer's old homestead (although we couldn't spot it) before a final long drop to a series of mossy stone walls – all that's left of abandoned homesteads. The trail rejoins the Caldwell Fork Trail for a 2.8-mile return.

After a storm, downed trees along the entire loop and washed-out footbridges on the Caldwell Fork Trail can turn this ramble into an epic adventure, so check the trail status with the camp host or read the signage at the trailhead after bad weather. On a couple of our creek crossings, the fast-flowing water hit above the knee and could prove dangerous with younger kids. If you have a hiking pole, bring it.

Rough Fork Trail to Woody Place   HIKING
( ) Families looking for an easy hike with a side of history should tackle this 2-mile out-and-back trail, which ribbons beneath white pines on an old road bed. Kids will enjoy scampering across the creek on foot logs. The house here began as a log cabin, which sheltered a family of 16 in the late 1860s. Frame additions are from the early 1900s.

After the Civil War, two families merged *Brady Bunch*–style in the home after widower Jonathan Woody married widow Mary Ann Caldwell. He moved into her log cabin with his five children. Nine of her 12 children were still living there. Good times!

If you're hiking solo, never mind those rumors about the Wild Man of Cataloochee. We're pretty sure this legendary backwoodsman died in 2010, but what was that sound over there...?

Little Cataloochee
Baptist Church   HIKING

(off Old NC 284) Built in 1889, this photogenic hilltop church in Little Cataloochee can only be reached on foot or horseback via the Little Cataloochee Trail, which stretches from Big Cataloochee to Old NC 284. The 4-mile, round-trip hike to the church from Old NC 284 passes the 1864 Hannah Cabin and the once-bustling community of Ola – now only whispers of its existence remain.

Inside the church you'll find a pot-bellied stove and white wooden pews. There's a graveyard at the base of the hill.

If hiking to the church from Big Cataloochee Valley, you'll follow the Pretty Hollow Gap Trail to the Little Cataloochee Trail. If you backtrack to Big Cataloochee after reaching the church, it's about 8 miles round trip. To hike the entire Little Cataloochee Trail from Big Cataloochee Valley to Old NC 284 (just over 6 miles one way), consider leaving a car at the trailhead on Old NC 284 so you can shuttle back to your starting point instead of backtracking.

🛏 Sleeping

Great Smoky Mountains National Park provides varied camping options. LeConte Lodge (p111) is the only place where you can get a room, however, and you have to hike to the top of a mountain to enjoy the privilege. Gatlinburg has the most sleeping options of any gateway town, though prices are high. Nearby Pigeon Forge, 10 miles north of Sugarlands Visitor Center, and Sevierville, 17 miles north, have cheaper options.

The National Park Service maintains developed campgrounds at nine locations in the park (a 10th remains closed indefinitely). Each campground has restrooms with cold running water and flush toilets, but there are no showers or electrical or water hookups in the park (though some campgrounds do have electricity for emergency

---

WORTH A TRIP

PIGEON FORGE, TENNESSEE

You can step aboard the *Titanic*, ride a 200ft-high Ferris wheel and plunge toward the earth on America's first 'wing coaster' in Pigeon Forge, a sprawling cacophony of excess and traffic burning bright in the shadow of the Great Smoky Mountains. With liquor by the drink available since 2013, the city has also loosened up a bit at night. Pigeon Forge is named in part for the Little Pigeon River, which flows through the action. Its banks were once a roosting spot for passenger pigeons – now extinct. Best known today as the home of Dollywood, Dolly Parton's namesake theme park, the city is packed tight with hotels, restaurants and family-friendly attractions.

Pigeon Forge is 8 miles from Great Smoky Mountains National Park, but traffic and stoplights can make that 8 miles seem a mighty long way.

Titanic Museum (☎ 417-334-9500; www.titanicpigeonforge.com; 2134 Parkway; adult $26, child 5-11yr $13; ⊙ 9am-10pm Jul & early Aug, closes earlier rest of the year; P) On April 15, 1912 the steamship Titanic sank on her maiden voyage after colliding with an iceberg. The ship's history and the stories of many of her passengers are shared through artifacts, black-and-white photographs, personal histories and thoughtful interactive displays. Highlights include an actual deck chair from the ship, a replica of the grand staircase and a haunting musical tribute to the ship's young musicians, who chose to stay onboard and play, possibly to keep passengers calm. All perished.

Great Smoky Mountain Wheel (☎ 865-286-0119; www.islandpigeonforge.com; 131 Island Dr; adult $14, child 3-11yr $9; ⊙ 10am-midnight late May-early Aug, varies rest of the year) One ticket gets you three spins inside an all-glass gondola on this 200ft-tall Ferris wheel, which anchors The Island amusement park. Views of the Great Smokies are breathtaking.

Dollywood (p41) Dollywood is a self-created ode to the patron saint of East Tennessee: the big-haired, big-bosomed and big-hearted country singer Dolly Parton. A clean and friendly place, the park features Appalachian-themed rides and attractions, the Splash Country water park, mountain crafts, Southern-fried restaurants and the DreamMore Resort.

situations). Each individual campsite has a fire grate and picnic table.

With the nine developed campgrounds offering more than 900 campsites, you'd think finding a place to pitch would be easy. Not so in the busy summer season, so plan ahead. Many sites can be reserved in advance, and several campgrounds (Cataloochee, Abrams Creek, Big Creek and Balsam Mountain) require advance reservations. Reserve through www.recreation.gov. Cades Cove and Smokemont campgrounds are open year-round; others are open March to October.

Backcountry camping is an excellent option, which is only chargeable up to five nights ($4 per night; after that, it's free). A permit is required. You can make reservations online at http://smokiespermits.nps.gov, and get permits at the ranger stations or visitor centers.

Be sure to review all campground regulations, which are available on the park website.

Balsam Mountain
CAMPGROUND $

(www.recreation.gov; Heintooga Ridge Rd; campsites $25; ☉mid-May–Oct) This small highlands campground is considered by many to be the park's most lovely, thanks to its privileged placement within an 'island' forest of red spruce and Fraser firs. Though the 46 campsites are somewhat small, the upside is that it discourages behemoth RVs from roosting (though RVs up to 30ft are allowed).

The campground is 8 miles from the Blue Ridge Parkway via Heintooga Ridge Rd.

Smokemont
CAMPGROUND $

(www.recreation.gov; Newfound Gap Rd; campsites $21-25) The Smokemont campground's 142 sites are the only North Carolina campsites open year-round. As with most other campgrounds in the park, there isn't much space between sites. At 2200ft elevation, Smokemont is situated beside the rushing mountain stream of Bradley Fork, although no sites directly overlook the water.

The campground is located just off Newfound Gap Rd, about 4 miles north of the Oconaluftee Visitor Center near the park's entrance by Cherokee, NC. This is a good base for hiking, with several trails leading off from the campground.

Elkmont
CAMPGROUND $

(☎865-436-1271; www.recreation.gov; Little River Rd; campsites $21-27; ☉early Mar-late Nov) The park's largest campground is on Little River Rd, 5 miles west of the Sugarlands Visitor Center. Little River and Jakes Creek run through this wooded campground and the sound of rippling water adds tranquility. There are 200 tent and RV campsites and 20 walk-in sites. All are reservable beginning May 15.

DON'T MISS

KNOXVILLE'S URBAN WILDERNESS

Dubbed a 'scruffy little city' by the *Wall Street Journal* before the 1982 World's Fair, Knoxville is strutting its stuff these days as an increasingly prominent and well-polished destination for outdoor, gastronomy and craft-beer enthusiasts. No longer content to play second fiddle to nearby Chattanooga and Asheville, the city – a former textiles production center – now touts itself as a base camp for visitors to Great Smoky Mountains National Park. Sugarlands Visitor Center (p105) is just 29 miles away.

For hikers and mountain bikers, the city's ever-expanding **Urban Wilderness** is becoming its own reason to visit. Just 3 miles from downtown South Knoxville, the Urban Wilderness is home to 50 miles of hiking and cycling trails. Parks, quarries and historic battlefields dot the more than 1000 forested acres – all linked by various trails. Highlights include **Baker Creek Preserve** (www.outdoorknoxville.com; 3700 Lancaster Ave), containing the region's only double-black-diamond mountain-bike trail, and **Mead's Quarry Lake** (☎865-696-0806; www.ijams.org; 2915 Island Home Ave; kayaks, canoes & SUPs per hr $12; ☉3-7pm Mon-Fri, 10am-6pm Sat, noon-6pm Sun Jun-Aug, reduced hr in fall & spring, closed winter), where you can rent canoes and paddleboards in warmer months. **Ijams Nature Center** (☎865-577-4717; www.ijams.org; 2915 Island Home Ave; ☉9am-5pm Mon-Sat, from 11am Sun; ⊞) doubles as the headquarters of the Urban Wilderness, and it should be your first stop. Download the Urban Wilderness mobile map app at www.outdoorknoxville.com for an overview.

Cades Cove Campground   CAMPGROUND $

(☑ 865-448-2472; www.recreation.gov; campsites $25) This woodsy campground with 159 sites is a great place to sleep if you want to get a jump on visiting Cades Cove. There's a store, drinking water and bathrooms, but no showers. There are 29 tent-only sites. Sites can be reserved in peak season – May 15 through October. The rest of the year, campsites are first-come, first served.

Cataloochee Campground   CAMPGROUND $

(☑ 877-444-6777; www.recreation.gov; Cataloochee Rd; campsites $25; ⊗ late Mar-Oct) This remote campground in a forest of hemlock and white pine has spacious campsites arranged off a loop road. Six of the 27 sites lie along the excellent fishing waters of Cataloochee Creek. Reservations are mandatory year-round, and the campground fills up on summer evenings. The campground host has brochures and maps.

Take exit 20 off I-40, go west on Hwy 276 to Cove Creek Rd and follow it to Cataloochee Rd.

★ LeConte Lodge   CABIN $$

(☑ 865-429-5704; www.lecontelodge.com; cabins incl breakfast & dinner adult $148, child 4-12yr $85; ⊗ mid-Mar–mid-Nov) The only non-camping accommodation in the park is LeConte Lodge. Though the only way to get to the lodge's rustic, electricity-free cabins is on five uphill hiking trails varying in length from 5.5 miles (Alum Cave Trail; p104) to 8.9 miles (Trillium Gap Trail), it's so popular you need to reserve many months in advance.

Reservations for the lodge open on October 1 for the following season, and are booked solid within two days (the most desirable dates fill up within a few hours). However, it's well worth putting your name on a wait list, as openings often become available.

If you score a spot, set out early to make the most of the experience. You can check out photos of past lodge life in the office and lounge, and climb to the very top of the mountain (a further 0.2 miles beyond the cabins). After a hearty meal in the evening, you can sit in rocking chairs and watch the stars come out, or adjourn to the lounge for board games, guitar strumming and browsing old *National Geographic* magazines by lamplight.

✗ Eating

Nuts and berries notwithstanding, there's nothing to eat in Great Smoky Mountains National Park, save for items from vending machines at Sugarlands Visitor Center (p105) and the meager offerings sold at the Cades Cove Campground store (☑ 865-448-9034; www.cadescovetrading.com; 10035 Campground Dr; ⊗ 9am-9pm late May-Oct, to 5pm Mar-May, Nov & late Dec). If you make the hike up to LeConte Lodge, you can purchase cookies, drinks and sack lunches (which means a bagel with cream cheese, beef summer sausage, trail mix and fruit leather). Dinner is included for those staying overnight.

Luckily, there are lots of restaurant options in the surrounding towns.

❶ Information

Sugarlands Visitor Center (p105) At the park's northern entrance near Gatlinburg.

Cades Cove Visitor Center (☑ 865-436-7318; www.nps.gov/grsm; Cades Cove Loop Rd; ⊗ 9am-7pm Apr-Aug, closes earlier Sep-Mar) Halfway up Cades Cove Loop Rd, 24 miles off Hwy 441 from the Gatlinburg entrance.

Oconaluftee Visitor Center (p101) At the park's southern entrance near Cherokee in North Carolina.

Clingmans Dome Visitor Station (☑ 865-436-1200; Clingmans Dome Rd; ⊗ 10am-6pm Apr-Oct, 9:30am-5pm Nov) Small, very busy center at the start of the paved path up to the Clingmans Dome lookout.

❶ Getting There & Away

The closest airports to the national park are **McGhee Tyson Airport** (☑ 865-342-3000; www.flyknoxville.com; 2055 Alcoa Hwy, Alcoa) near Knoxville (40 miles northwest of Sugarlands Visitor Center) and Asheville Regional Airport (p95), 58 miles east of the Oconaluftee Visitor Center. Further afield you'll find **Chattanooga Metropolitan Airport** (CHA; ☑ 423-855-2202; www.chattairport.com; 1001 Airport Rd), 140 miles southwest of the park, Charlotte Douglas International Airport (p116), 170 miles east, and **Hartsfield-Jackson International Airport** (ATL; ☑ 800-897-1910; www.atl.com) in Atlanta (175 miles south of the park).

After you fly in, you'll need a car as there's no public transportation to the park. There's a wide variety of car-rental outfits at each of the airports.

Flights, cars and tours can be booked online at lonelyplanet.com/bookings.

CHARLOTTE

📞 704 / POP 859,400

North Carolina's largest city, Charlotte sprawls 15 miles in every direction from its compact, high-rise core. Futuristic skyscrapers pepper downtown Charlotte, which is officially known as 'Uptown,' supposedly because it sits on a barely visible ridge, but really because the council decided that sounds cooler. Uptown holds several fine museums plus the high-octane Nascar Hall of Fame, while more museums and historic sites are scattered further afield. Hotels and restaurants are also concentrated Uptown, though funkier neighborhoods within easy reach include Plaza Midwood, just east, with its boutiques and restaurants, and hip NoDa, along North Davidson St, where former textile mills hold breweries and cafes.

Named after the wife of George III – hence its nickname, the Queen City – Charlotte boomed when gold was discovered nearby, and later prospered from cotton and textiles. Having pioneered interstate banking in the 1980s, it's now the third-largest banking center in the US.

👁 Sights & Activities

Levine Museum of the New South   MUSEUM

(www.museumofthenewsouth.org; 200 E 7th St; adult/child 6-18yr $9/5; ☉10am-5pm Mon-Sat, from noon Sun; 🅿) Tracing the story of the 'New South' that emerged from the ashes of the Civil War, this committed museum explores the years of Reconstruction, Jim Crow and the Civil Rights movement. Haunting Dorothea Lange photos illuminate the Depression era on North Carolina's plantations, while changing exhibits highlight current issues such as the 2016 shooting of Keith Lamont Scott by police. Visitors are encouraged to respond to questions such as 'Does everyone have equal rights in the South today?'

Tip: they validate two hours of parking at the 7th Street Station garage next door.

Mint Museum Randolph   MUSEUM

(📞704-337-2000; www.mintmuseum.org; 2730 Randolph Rd; adult/child 5-17yr $15/6, 5-9pm Wed free; ☉11am-9pm Wed, to 6pm Thu-Sat, 1-5pm Sun; 🅿) The US Mint opened its first-ever outpost in Uptown Charlotte in 1837, using gold mined from the mountains nearby. Transported 3 miles southeast a century later, the building now holds treasures ranging from ceramic masterpieces from Britain and North Carolina to stunning modern American decorative glasswork. Best of all are the wonderful pre-Columbian artifacts created by the Aztecs and Maya.

Admission tickets also cover the Mint Museum Uptown (📞704-337-2000; www.mint museum.org; 500 S Tryon St; ☉11am-9pm Wed, to 6pm Thu-Sat, 1-5pm Sun), and are valid for two days.

Bechtler Museum of Modern Art   MUSEUM

(📞704-353-9200; www.bechtler.org; 420 S Tryon St; adult/child 11-18yr $8/4; ☉10am-5pm Mon & Wed-Sat, from noon Sun) An Uptown landmark, thanks to sculptor Niki de Saint Phalle's huge mirror-tiled *Firebird* out front, this showcase for 20th-century art was donated to the city by the Bechtlers, a family of Swiss industrialists. Highlights of its permanent collection, displayed on the 3rd floor, include ceramics and lithographs by Picasso, and tiny gilded bronzes by Alberto Giacometti, a family friend.

Look out for top-class temporary exhibitions on the 2nd and 4th floors.

⭐ US National Whitewater Center   ADVENTURE SPORTS

(📞704-391-3900; www.usnwc.org; 5000 Whitewater Center Pkwy; all-sport day pass adult/child under 10yr $59/49, individual activities $25, 3hr canopy tour $89; ☉dawn-dusk) A beyond-awesome hybrid of nature center and water park, this 1300-acre facility is home to the largest artificial white-water river in the world. You can paddle its rapids – which serve as training grounds for Olympic canoeists and kayakers – as part of a guided rafting trip, or enjoy a range of other adventure activities.

As well as several rope courses, an outdoor rock-climbing wall, paddle surfing and ziplines, it holds miles of wooded hiking and mountain-biking trails. Or you could just sip a craft brew while you watch the kayaks in action from the Pump House Biergarten. The center is 14 miles west of Charlotte. Parking costs $6.

🛏 Sleeping

Duke Mansion   INN $$

(📞704-714-4400; www.dukemansion.com; 400 Hermitage Rd; r $121-341; 🅿❄🛜) The century-old former home of the Duke family, including legendary heiress Doris Duke, is now a delightful B&B inn. Set in wooded gardens in the attractive Myers Park neighborhood, a couple of miles south of Uptown, it holds 20

CHEROKEE NATIONAL FOREST: WATERFALLS AND WHITE-WATER RAFTING

Hiding in plain sight along the eastern border of Tennessee, but overshadowed by Great Smoky Mountains National Park, 650,000-acre Cherokee National Forest (www.fs.usda. gov/cherokee) is chock-full of outdoor adventures and stunning scenery. Here, white-water rafters careen through class IV rapids on wild rivers, mountain bikers tear through the trees on singletrack trails, and day hikers stop and smell the wildflowers after rock-hopping across burbling streams.

Divided into northern and southern sections, which are separated by the national park, the forest is home to four ranger districts and 15 recreational zones. The Ocoee District is the best known of the districts, impressing visitors with a scenic byway, two vast trail networks and top-tier rafting on the Ocoee River. Many attractions are convenient to both eastern Tennessee and western North Carolina.

Hiking

Hundreds of miles of trails are open to hikers, with some of the best day hikes leading to waterfalls. Scenic meadows, called balds, blanket mountain ridges along the Appalachian Trail (AT), which crosses the forest on its run between Georgia and Maine.

Margarette Falls Trail (www.fs.usda.gov; Shelton Mission Rd) Good for families, dog walkers and waterfall junkies, this easy-to-moderate hike is a gorgeous half-day adventure for folks who want to explore the northern section of Cherokee National Forest. The 2.7-mile round-trip hike is steep and rocky in parts, with a few minor stream crossings, but the reward is sweet: a 60ft-high fan-shaped waterfall. Leashed pets are okay.

Benton Falls Trail (www.fs.usda.gov; Forest Road 77, Chilhowee Recreation Area; day-use per vehicle $3) This 3-mile out-and-back hike, which is part of the Chilhowee Trail System, follows a blue-blazed path through the woods, then ends with a steep but short drop to the base of dramatic 65ft-tall falls.

White-water Rafting

A handful of powerful rivers crash through the foothills. Rafting companies guide trips on these rivers in both the north and south sections of the forest. The Nantahala Outdoor Center (p100), which has outposts across eastern Tennessee, western North Carolina and northern Georgia, leads rafting trips on the Ocoee, French Broad and Pigeon Rivers.

---

light-filled rooms. Many still have their original tiled bathrooms, and some upstairs open onto their own screened sections of porch.

Rates include a buffet breakfast; there's no on-site restaurant, but there are dining options within walking distance.

★ **Ivey's Hotel** BOUTIQUE HOTEL $$$
(☎704-228-1111; www.theiveyshotel.com; 127 N Tryon St; r $299-499; P@🛜🐾) The Ivey's 42 Parisian-inspired rooms – all on the 2nd floor of a 1924 department-store building – are steeped in history (the 400-year-old oak-wood floors were sourced from a French winery) but have modern flair (55in Sony TVs, Bose soundbars). The balcony executive corner suites, awash in natural-light-sucking windows and exposed brick, are divine.

Crown-molded doors and hallways, unique watch-face art, Frette linens, custom-

designed furniture – the meticulously curated decor leaves no detail to chance.

✖ Eating

Price's Chicken Coop SOUTHERN US $
(☎704-333-9866; www.priceschickencoop.com; 1614 Camden Rd; mains $3.25-12.25; ⊙10am-6pm Tue-Sat) A timeless throwback in ever-gentrifying South End, this scruffy, cash-only takeout is a true Charlotte institution, regularly making 'Best Fried Chicken in America' lists. Order your 'dark quarter' or 'white half' from the white-jacketed cooks, then carry your bounty outside and start looking for a place to eat – leafy Latta Park is 10 minutes' walk east on Park Ave.

7th Street Public Market FOOD HALL $
(☎704-230-4346; www.7thstreetpublicmarket. com; 224 E 7th St; mains $10-15; ⊙7am-8pm Mon-

Thu, 7am-9pm Fri, 8:30am-9pm Sat, 8:30am-5pm Sun) This food hall's aromatic, irresistible kitchens and cafes entice Uptown palates with everything from gourmet coffee and craft beer to imported cheese and specialties from Orvieto, Italy. Pick a roasted-broccoli burger here, a raw cold-pressed juice there, and settle down at the central tables to enjoy.

Amélie's French Bakery & Cafe　CAFE $
(☎704-899-0088; www.ameliesfrenchbakery. com; 380 S College St; pastries $1-6, sandwiches $6.50; ⊗7am-10pm Mon-Thu, to midnight Fri & Sat, to 8pm Sun; 🖘) This new, shiny and very big outlet of a much-loved local bakery chain is the perfect spot to rest your feet or meet friends Uptown. The sandwiches and toasted tartines are great value, but it's the decadently voluptuous pastries that draw the crowds, from the simple almond cake known as a *financier* to the house version of a brioche.

Their vintage-styled original branch, at 2424 N Davidson St in the NoDa neighborhood, stays open 24 hours.

Mert's Heart & Soul　SOUTHERN US $
(☎704-342-4222; www.mertscharlotte.com; 214 N College St; mains $11-16; ⊗11am-9pm Mon-Fri, 9am-11:30pm Sat, 9am-9:30pm Sun) At street level, beneath Uptown's soaring skyscrapers, this cozy, homely diner buzzes with bankers and bohos alike. Its Lowcountry classics include shrimp and grits, barbecue beef ribs and fried catfish, but we love the spicy salmon cakes best.

★Soul Gastrolounge Tapas　SUSHI, SANDWICHES $$
(☎704-348-1848; www.soulgastrolounge.com; 1500 Central Ave; small plates $7-20, sushi $4-14, sandwiches $9-15; ⊗5pm-2am) This sultry but welcoming Plaza Midwood speakeasy serves a globally inspired selection of small plates, ranging from skewers and sushi rolls to Cu-

Charlotte

ban and Vietnamese sandwiches. Each little gem is infused with unique, satisfying flavors. The dancing tuna rolls, with jalapeños and two spicy mayos, are highly recommended.

With no reservations, the wait can be maddening – 187 minutes for us! But they use the NoWait app (http://nowait.com), so you can pass that time in a few breweries.

Halcyon Flavors from the Earth   AMERICAN $$

(☑ 704-910-0865; www.halcyonflavors.com; 500 S Tryon St; salads & sandwiches $11-18, mains $32-44; ⊙ 11am-10pm Tue-Sat, to 3pm Sun) A perfect people-watching perch overlooking the Uptown bustle, the Mint Museum's light-filled restaurant is ideal for a zestful lunch or more substantial (and expensive) dinner. Ingredients sourced from local farmers are prominent on the changing daily menu, with the likes of kale or brussels-sprout salads and pork-belly BLTs. Dinner mains might include saddle of rabbit and halibut with crab soufflé.

Asbury   SOUTHERN US $$$

(☑ 704-342-1193; www.theasbury.com; 235 N Tryon St; sandwiches $8-14, mains $20-38; ⊙ 11am-10pm Mon-Fri, from 5pm Sat & Sun) Uptown's finest dining is to be had in the Dunhill Hotel's restaurant, opening straight onto Tryon St. Rooted in Carolinian classics, but given a contemporary makeover, chef Matthew Krenz' cuisine ranges from sorghum-glazed duck with walnut and garlic gremolata to simpler staples, served anytime, such as mac, cheese and country ham.

🍷 Drinking & Nightlife

The Queen City has acquired a phenomenal number of breweries in recent years, with 25 in the city proper at last count, and another 20 or so in the metropolitan area. Several of the best line North Davidson St, while there's another concentration in South End.

★ NoDa Brewing Company   MICROBREWERY

(☑ 704-900-6851; www.nodabrewing.com; 2921 N Tryon St; ⊙ 4-9pm Mon-Thu, 4-10pm Fri, noon-10pm Sat, noon-7pm Sun; 🛜) Charlotte's best craft-beer playground is hidden behind NoDa's new and easy-to-overlook North End brewery. We went up on a Friday night and it looked abandoned. At the back, however, we found a packed playhouse of brews (pints $4 to $7) and boccie ball, plus cornhole, Frisbee golf, a fire pit, a massive patio and Charlotte's top food truck, Tin Kitchen.

Wooden Robot   MICROBREWERY

(www.woodenrobotbrewery.com; 1440 S Tryon St; ⊙ 4-10pm Tue-Thu, 3pm-midnight Fri, noon-midnight Sat, noon-9pm Sun; 🛜) One of Charlotte's most sociable taprooms – when the South End scene descends, it can feel like a sophisticated singles bar, full of hot millennials – this was voted the city's best by Untappd users. It's all brick and beautiful hardwoods and serious suds, often brewed with local coffee, chocolate, malt and syrups (small/medium/large beer from $2/4/6).

Heist Brewery   MICROBREWERY

(☑ 704-375-8260; www.heistbrewery.com; 2909 N Davidson St; ⊙ 11am-midnight Mon-Wed, to 2am Thu-Sat, 10am-midnight Sun; 🛜) Set in a former mill, Heist is one of several good-time NoDa breweries. With 36 taps spread over three bars (pints from $4.50), it offers some exceptionally juicy IPAs, craft cocktails ($9 to $13) and an extensive menu of inventive, farm-to-table pub food (dinner mains $10 to $16).

The beer focus is on small-batch Belgians, saisons, imperial IPAs and stouts.

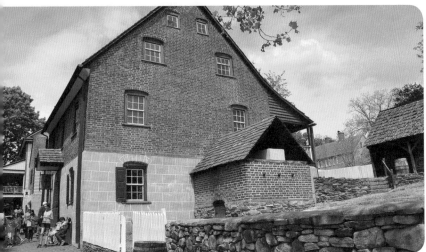

Winkler Bakery, Old Salem

ℹ Information

Charlotte's main **visitor center** (☑ 800-231-4636; www.charlottesgotalot.com; 501 S College St, Charlotte Convention Center; ⊙ 9am-5pm Mon-Sat) is in Uptown. There's also an information desk at the airport.

ℹ Getting There & Away

Charlotte Douglas International Airport (CLT; ☑ 704-359-4013; www.cltairport.com; 5501 Josh Birmingham Pkwy), 7 miles west of Uptown, is an American Airlines hub that welcomes nonstop flights from continental Europe and the UK. Both the **Greyhound** (☑ 704-372-0456; www.greyhound.com; 601 W Trade St) and **Amtrak** (www.amtrak.com; 1914 N Tryon St) stations are handy to Uptown.

WINSTON-SALEM

☑ 336 / POP 242,203

In its tobacco-processing heyday, a century ago, Winston-Salem was the largest city in North Carolina. Since then, the city that gave the world Camel cigarettes (and Krispy Kreme doughnuts!) has slipped back to fifth place, leaving its pocket-sized downtown looking a little faded but charming nonetheless. For visitors, though, the big attraction lies immediately south, in the verdant streets of Salem ('peace') itself, founded in 1766 by German Protestants from the Moravian sect. Their settlement remains remarkably intact, despite the encroachment of the nearby industrial city of Winston, which by 1913 had crept so close that there was only just room to squeeze a hyphen between the two, and create Winston-Salem.

⊙ Sights

★**Old Salem** HISTORIC SITE
(☑ 336-721-7350; www.oldsalem.org; 900 Old Salem Rd; all-in-one ticket adult/child under 19yr Tue-Sat $27/13, Sun $22/11, 2-stop ticket Tue-Sat $18/9; ⊙ 9:30am-4:30pm Tue-Sat, from 1pm Sun; ℗) The beautifully preserved core of the Moravian settlement of Salem extends across several blocks south of downtown. You're not obliged to pay for admission if you simply want to admire the architecture, eat in the Tavern, or shop in the wonderful **Winkler Bakery** or various craft shops. You'll have a much richer experience, though, if you pay for access to the on-site museums, houses and workshops, where costumed guides explain and demonstrate Moravian traditions, such as gardening, doctoring and gunsmithing.

If you plan to visit any of the paying attractions, start by buying tickets at the large modern **visitor center**, across the main road from Old Salem proper, at the southern end of a large parking lot. And if your time is short, prioritize the Museum of Early Southern Decorative Arts and the rewarding displays on Salem's African American population in and around **St Philips Church**.

Museum of Early Southern Decorative Arts
MUSEUM

(☎ 336-721-7369; www.mesda.org; 924 S Main St, Old Salem; all-in-one ticket adult/child under 19yr Tue-Sat $27/13, Sun $22/11, two-stop ticket Tue-Sat $18/9; ⏰ 9:30am-4:30pm Tue-Sat, from 1pm Sun; P) Only accessible with combined admission to Old Salem's other historic sites, this showpiece museum extends way beyond the local Moravian heritage to celebrate arts and crafts from the seven states of the early South. As well as paintings and prints, it's especially strong on furniture, ceramics and woodwork.

Buying the 'two-stop' option grants admission to this and one other sight.

Reynolda House Museum of American Art
MUSEUM

(☎ 336-758-5150; www.reynoldahouse.org; 2250 Reynolda Rd; adult/child under 19yr $18/free; ⏰ 9:30am-4:30pm Tue-Sat, from 1:30pm Sun; P) Tobacco magnate RJ Reynolds started operations in Winston-Salem in 1875, and the family business prospered through world-beating brands including Camel (introduced 1913) and Winston (1954). Bathed in natural light, the rather lovely house he built in 1917 – they call it a bungalow, despite the presence of both an attic and a basement – now holds a small collection of art, including an incongruous video installation by Nam June Paik.

🛏 Sleeping & Eating

Kimpton Cardinal
HOTEL $$

(☎ 336-724-1009; www.thecardinalhotel.com; 51 E 4th St; r from $170; 🛜) Downtown's classiest hotel opened in 2016, in the refurbished RJ Reynolds building downtown, a 1929 art deco structure that served as the prototype for the Empire State Building, built two years later. The public spaces are magnificent, and, as well as almost 200 rooms in hip contemporary style, it holds an adult playroom, complete with spiral slide and bowling alley.

The Zevely Inn
B&B $$

(☎ 336-748-9299; http://zevelyinn.com; 803 S Main St, Old Salem; r/ste from $159/299; 🛜) The only lodging option in the peaceful historic

neighborhood of Old Salem belonged to the city mayor during the 1840s. Now a B&B, its exquisitely preserved features include a wonderful mural in the dining room; the guest rooms, all en-suite, vary in size, and offer amenities such as fireplaces and four-poster beds. Rates include a hot buffet breakfast.

Sweet Potatoes
SOUTHERN US $

(☎ 336-727-4844; www.sweetpotatoes.ws; 607 N Trade St; lunch mains $7-16, dinner mains $14-22; ⏰ 11am-3pm & 5-10pm Tue-Sat, 10:30am-3pm Sun) They don't take reservations at this hugely popular 'Southern gourmet' restaurant in the Arts District downtown, but it's worth waiting in line to enjoy classic dishes including fried green tomatoes, catfish or chicken – let alone dinner mains such as Gullah shrimp and crab pilau. And leave room for their trademark sweet potatoes.

★ Tavern in Old Salem
SOUTHERN US $$

(☎ 336-722-1227; www.thetaverninoldsalem.ws; 736 S Main St, Old Salem; lunch mains $10, dinner mains $18-25; ⏰ 11am-3:30pm & 5-9pm Tue-Sat, 11am-3pm Sun) At lunchtime, Old Salem visitors wait patiently in line for waitstaff in old Moravian dress to serve old-time favorites, including pot roast, grilled bratwurst and our favorite, the beer cheese soup. In the evening, the open back porch comes into its own, the ambience turns more formal and romantic, and the menu more contemporary, with a fine list of cocktails.

🍷 Drinking & Nightlife

Foothills Brewpub
MICROBREWERY

(☎ 336-777-3348; www.foothillsbrewing.com; 638 W 4th St; ⏰ 11am-midnight Sun-Tue, to 2am Wed-Sat) The downtown outlet of Winston-Salem's best-known microbrewery features a dozen seasonally changing favorites on tap. It also has a good menu of pub food (mains $13 to $21), such as fish 'n' chips and barbecued ribs.

❶ Getting There & Away

Winston-Salem is roughly equidistant from Charlotte Douglas International Airport (p116), 83 miles southwest, and Raleigh-Durham International Airport (p82), 94 miles east.

Driving in the USA

With a comprehensive network of interstate highways, enthusiastic car culture and jaw-dropping scenery, the USA is an ideal road-tripping destination, even year-round in some spots.

Driving Fast Facts

Right or left? Drive on the right

Legal driving age Virginia: 16 years & 3 months; North Carolina: 16 years & 6 months

Top speed limit 70mph on some highways

Best bumper sticker POO (Peaks of Otter, VA)

DRIVER'S LICENSE & DOCUMENTS

All US drivers must carry a valid driver's license from their home state, proof of vehicle insurance and their vehicle's registration papers or a copy of their vehicle-rental contract.

Foreign drivers can legally drive in the USA for 12 months using their home driver's license. An International Driving Permit (IDP) isn't required, but will have more credibility with traffic police and will simplify the car-rental process, especially if your home license isn't in English and/or doesn't have a photo. International automobile associations issue IDPs, valid for one year, for a fee. Always carry your home license with your IDP.

To ride a motorcycle in the USA, you will need either a valid US state motorcycle license or an IDP specially endorsed for motorcycles.

The American Automobile Association (AAA) has reciprocal agreements with some international auto clubs (eg Canada's CAA, AA in the UK). Bring your membership card from home.

INSURANCE

Liability All drivers are required to obtain a minimum amount of liability insurance, which would cover the damage that you might cause to other people and property in case of an accident. Liability insurance can be purchased from rental-car companies for about $12 per day.

Collision For damage to the rental vehicle, a collision damage waiver (CDW) is available from the rental company for about $18 a day.

Alternative sources Your personal auto insurance may extend to rental cars, so it's worth investigating before purchasing liability or collision from the rental company. Additionally, some credit cards offer reimbursement coverage for collision damages if you rent the car with that credit card; again, check before departing. Most credit-card coverage isn't valid for rentals of more than 15 days or for exotic models, SUVs, vans and 4WD vehicles.

RENTING A VEHICLE

To rent your own wheels, you'll usually need to be at least 25 years old, hold a valid driver's license and have a major credit card, *not* a check or debit card.

Cars

Rental car rates generally include unlimited mileage, but expect surcharges for additional drivers and one-way rentals. Airport locations may have cheaper base rates but higher add-on fees. If you get a fly-drive package, local taxes may be extra when you pick up the car. Child and infant safety seats are legally required; reserve them (around $10 per day, or $50 per trip) when booking your car.

Some major car-rental companies offer 'green' fleets of hybrid or alternative-fuel rental cars, but they're in short supply. Make reservations far in advance and expect to pay significantly more for these models. Many companies rent vans with wheelchair lifts and hand-controlled vehicles at no extra cost, but you must also reserve these well in advance.

International car-rental companies with hundreds of branches nationwide include:

Alamo (www.alamo.com)

Avis (www.avis.com)

Budget (www.budget.com)

Dollar (www.dollar.com)

Enterprise (www.enterprise.com)

Fox (www.foxrentacar.com)

Hertz (www.hertz.com)

National (www.nationalcar.com)

Thrifty (www.thrifty.com)

To find local and independent car-rental companies, check:

Car Rental Express (www.carrentalexpress.com) Search for independent car-rental companies and specialty cars (eg hybrids).

Rent-a-Wreck (www.rentawreck.com) Often rents to younger drivers (over-18s) and those without credit cards; ask about long-term rentals.

If you don't mind no-cancellation policies or which company you rent from, you may find better deals on car rentals through online travel discounters such as **Priceline** (www.priceline.com) and **Hotwire** (www.hotwire.com).

Motorcycles

Motorcycle rentals and insurance are very expensive, with steep surcharges for one-way rentals. Discounts may be available for three-day and weekly rentals.

Road Trip Websites

AUTO CLUBS

American Automobile Association (www.aaa.com) Roadside assistance, travel discounts, trip planning and maps for members.

Better World Club (www.betterworldclub.com) Eco-friendly alternative to AAA.

MAPS

America's Byways (www.fhwa.dot.gov/byways) Inspiring itineraries, maps and directions for scenic drives.

Google Maps (http://maps.google.com) Turn-by-turn driving directions with estimated traffic delays.

Waze (www.waze.com) Popular, free, crowdsourced traffic and navigation app.

GasBuddy (www.gasbuddy.com) Website and app that finds the cheapest places to gas up nearby.

ROAD CONDITIONS & CLOSURES

US Department of Transportation (www.fhwa.dot.gov/trafficinfo) Links to state and local road conditions, traffic and weather.

Blue Ridge Parkway (www.nps.gov/blri)

Shenandoah National Park (www.nps.gov/shen)

Driving Problem-Buster

What should I do if my car breaks down? Put on your hazard lights (flashers) and carefully pull over to the side of the road. Call the roadside emergency assistance number for your auto club or rental-car company. Otherwise, call information (✐411) for the number of the nearest towing service or auto-repair shop.

What if I have an accident? If you're safely able to do so, move your vehicle out of traffic and onto the road's shoulder. For minor collisions with no major property damage or bodily injuries, be sure to exchange driver's license and auto-insurance information with the other driver, then file a report with your insurance provider or notify your car-rental company as soon as possible. For major accidents, call ✐911 and wait for the police and emergency services to arrive.

What should I do if I'm stopped by the police? Don't get out of the car unless asked. Keep your hands where the officer can see them (ie on the steering wheel). Always be courteous. Most fines for traffic or parking violations can be handled by mail or online within a 30-day period.

What happens if my car gets towed? Call the local non-emergency police number and ask where to pick up your car. Towing and vehicle storage fees accumulate quickly, up to hundreds of dollars for just a few hours or a day, so act promptly.

National rental outfitters include:

Eagle Rider (www.eaglerider.com) Motorcycle rentals and tours in more than 25 states, including Virginia, and Washington, DC.

Harley-Davidson (www.harley-davidson.com) Links to scores of local motorcycle shops that rent Harleys.

RVs & Campervans

Popular with road-trippers, recreational vehicles (RVs, also called motorhomes) are cumbersome to drive and burn fuel at an alarming rate. They do solve transportation, accommodation and self-catering kitchen needs in one fell swoop. Even so, there are many places in national parks and scenic areas (eg narrow mountain roads) where they can't be driven.

Make reservations for RVs and smaller campervans as far in advance as possible. Rental costs vary by size and model; basic rates often don't include mileage, bedding or kitchen kits, vehicle prep and cleaning or additional taxes and fees. If bringing pets is allowed, a surcharge may apply.

National rental agencies include:

Cruise America (www.cruiseamerica.com) With 125 RV rental locations nationwide.

El Monte RV (www.elmonterv.com) RV rentals in more than 25 states, including Virginia, North Carolina and Tennessee.

MAPS

Tourist information offices and visitor centers distribute free but often very basic maps. GPS navigation can't be relied upon everywhere, notably in thick forests and remote mountain areas. If you're planning on doing a lot of driving, you may want a more detailed fold-out road map or map atlas, such as those published by Rand McNally (www.randmcnally.com). Members of the AAA and its international auto-club affiliates can pick up free maps at AAA branch offices nationwide.

For an interactive online map covering the entire Blue Ridge Parkway, check out www.blueridgeparkway.org/parkway-map, produced by the Blue Ridge Parkway Association (BRPA). From the BRPA website you can also download the Blue Ridge Parkway Travel Planner app, which has maps.

ROAD CONDITIONS

The USA's highways are not always perfect ribbons of unblemished asphalt. Common road hazards include potholes, rockfalls, mudslides, flooding, fog, free-ranging livestock and wildlife, commuter traffic jams on weekday mornings and afternoons, and drivers distracted by technology, kids and pets or blinded by road rage.

ROAD DISTANCES (miles)

	Abingdon	Asheville	Brevard	Charlotte	Charlottesville	Gatlinburg	Knoxville	Richmond	Roanoke	Staunton	Washington
Asheville	111										
Brevard	143	34									
Charlotte	194	125	126								
Charlottesville	241	351	383	270							
Gatlinburg	130	81	105	197	370						
Knoxville	127	115	139	231	367	34					
Richmond	309	373	404	289	71	438	435				
Roanoke	134	244	276	196	121	262	260	189			
Staunton	208	318	350	272	40	337	335	108	88		
Washington	354	471	503	397	117	489	487	109	241	157	
Winston-Salem	146	145	176	78	210	224	258	229	105	192	337

In places where winter driving is an issue, snow tires and tire chains may be necessary, especially in the mountains. Ideally, carry your own chains and learn how to use them before you hit the road. Driving off-road or on dirt roads is often forbidden by rental-car contracts, and it can be very dangerous in wet weather. In winter, sections of the Blue Ridge Parkway are often closed due to snowy and icy conditions. Skyline Drive in Shenandoah National Park may also close due to inclement weather.

Major highways, expressways and bridges in some urban areas require paying tolls. Sometimes tolls can be paid using cash (bills or coins), but occasionally an electronic toll-payment sensor is required. If you don't have one, your vehicle's license plate will likely be photographed and you'll be billed later, usually at a higher rate. Ask about this when picking up your rental vehicle to avoid surprising surcharges on your final bill after you've returned the car.

ROAD RULES

➡ Drive on the right-hand side of the road.
➡ Talking or texting on a cell (mobile) phone while driving is illegal in most states.

➡ The maximum legal blood-alcohol concentration for drivers is 0.08%. Penalties for 'DUI' (driving under the influence of alcohol or drugs) are severe, including heavy fines, driver's license suspension, court appearances and/or jail time.Police may give roadside sobriety checks to assess if you've been drinking or using drugs. If you fail, they'll require you to take a breath, urine or blood test to determine the level of drugs and alcohol in your body. Refusing to be tested is treated the same as if you'd taken the test and failed.

➡ The use of seat belts and infant and child safety seats is legally required nationwide, although exact regulations vary by state.

➡ Wearing motorcycle helmets is mandatory in many states, and always a good idea.

➡ High-occupancy vehicle (HOV) lanes marked with a diamond symbol are reserved for cars with multiple occupants, but sometimes only during specific, signposted hours.

➡ Unless otherwise posted, the speed limit is generally 55mph or 65mph on highways, 25mph to 35mph in cities and towns and as low as 15mph in school zones. It's illegal to pass a school bus when its lights are flashing.

Blue Ridge Parkway Playlist

Keep on the Sunny Side The Carter Family

Go on Lovin' Dori Freeman

Home Across the Blue Ridge Mountains Doc Watson

Hit 'Em up Style Carolina Chocolate Drops

Wagon Wheel Old Crow Medicine Show

Coat of Many Colors Dolly Parton

➡ Except where signs prohibit doing so, turning right at a red light after coming to a full stop is usually permitted.(one notable exception is New York City). Intersecting cross-traffic still has the right of way, however.

➡ At four-way stop signs, cars proceed in order of arrival. If two cars arrive simultaneously, the one on the right goes first. When in doubt, politely wave the other driver ahead.

➡ At intersections, U-turns may be legal unless otherwise posted, but this varies by state.

➡ When emergency vehicles approach from either direction, carefully pull over to the side of the road.

➡ In many states, it's illegal to carry open containers of alcohol (even if they're empty) inside a vehicle. Unless the containers are full and still sealed, put them in the trunk instead.

➡ Most states have strict anti-littering laws; throwing trash from a vehicle may incur a $1000 fine. Besides, it's bad for the environment.

➡ Hitchhiking is illegal in some states, and restricted in others.

PARKING

Free parking is plentiful in small towns and rural areas, but scarce and often expensive in cities. Municipal parking meters and centralized pay stations usually accept coins and credit or debit cards. Parking at broken meters is often prohibited; where allowed, the posted time limit still applies.

When parking on the street, carefully read all posted regulations and restrictions (eg 30-minute maximum, no parking during scheduled street-cleaning hours) and pay attention to colored curbs, or you may be ticketed and towed. In many towns and cities, overnight street parking is prohibited downtown and in designated areas reserved for local residents with permits.

At city parking garages and lots, expect to pay at least $2 per hour and $10 to $45 for all-day or overnight parking. For valet parking at hotels, restaurants, nightclubs etc, a flat fee of $5 to $40 is typically charged. Tip the valet attendant at least $2 when your keys are handed back to you.

FUEL

Many gas stations in the USA have fuel pumps with automated credit-card pay screens. Some machines ask for your ZIP code after you swipe your card. For foreign travelers, or those with cards issued outside the US, you'll have to pay inside before fueling up. Just indicate how much you'd like to put on the card. If there's still credit left over after you fuel up, pop back inside and the attendant will put the difference back on your card.

SAFETY

Vehicle theft, break-ins and vandalism are a problem mostly in urban areas, although smash-and-grab thefts may occur at remote hiking trailheads. Be sure to lock your vehicle's doors, leave the windows rolled up and use any anti-theft devices that have been installed (eg car alarm, steering-wheel lock). Do not leave any valuables visible inside your vehicle; instead, stow them in the trunk before arriving at your destination, or else take them with you once you've parked.

BEHIND THE SCENES

SEND US YOUR FEEDBACK

We love to hear from travelers – your comments help make our books better. We read every word, and we guarantee that your feedback goes straight to the authors. Visit **lonelyplanet. com/contact** to submit your updates and suggestions.

Note: We may edit, reproduce and incorporate your comments in Lonely Planet products such as guidebooks, websites and digital products, so let us know if you don't want your comments reproduced or your name acknowledged. For a copy of our privacy policy visit lonelyplanet.com/privacy.

ACKNOWLEDGMENTS

Climate map data adapted from Peel MC, Finlayson BL & McMahon TA (2007) 'Updated World Map of the Köppen-Geiger Climate Classification', Hydrology and Earth System Sciences, 11, 163344.

Cover photographs: Front: view from Waterrock Knob, Blue Ridge Parkway, NaturalStock/Shutterstock ©; Back: Mabry Mill, Crooked Road, anthony heflin/Shutterstock ©

THIS BOOK

This 1st edition of *Blue Ridge Parkway Road Trips* was researched and written by Amy C Balfour, Virginia Maxwell, Regis St Louis and Greg Ward. This guidebook was produced by the following:

Destination Editor Trisha Ping

Product Editor Barbara Delissen

Cartographer Valentina Kremenchutskaya

Regional Senior Cartographer Alison Lyall

Senior Product Editor Vicky Smith

Book Designers Fergal Condon, Mazzy Prinsep

Assisting Editors Andrew Bain, James Bainbridge, Carly Hall

Cover Researcher Naomi Parker

Thanks to Andrea Dobbin, Anne Mason, Wibowo Rusli, Angela Tinson

OUR STORY

A beat-up old car, a few dollars in the pocket and a sense of adventure. In 1972 that's all Tony and Maureen Wheeler needed for the trip of a lifetime – across Europe and Asia overland to Australia. It took several months, and at the end – broke but inspired – they sat at their kitchen table writing and stapling together their first travel guide, *Across Asia on the Cheap*. Within a week they'd sold 1500 copies. Lonely Planet was born.

Today, Lonely Planet has offices in Franklin, London, Melbourne, Oakland, Dublin, Beijing and Delhi, with more than 600 staff and writers. We share Tony's belief that 'a great guidebook should do three things: inform, educate and amuse'.

INDEX

000 Map pages

S

T

U

V

W

OUR WRITERS

AMY C BALFOUR

Amy practiced law in Virginia before moving to Los Angeles to try to break in as a screenwriter. After a stint as a writer's assistant on *Law & Order*, she jumped into freelance writing, focusing on travel, food and the outdoors. She has hiked, biked and paddled across Southern California and the Southwest. She recently criss-crossed the Great Plains in search of the region's best burgers and barbecue.

VIRGINIA MAXWELL

Although based in Australia, Virginia spends at least half of her year updating Lonely Planet destination coverage across the globe. The Mediterranean is her major area of interest – she has covered Spain, Italy, Turkey, Syria, Lebanon, Israel, Egypt, Morocco and Tunisia for LP – but she also covers Finland, Bali, Armenia, the Netherlands, the US and Australia for LP products. Follow her @maxwellvirginia on Instagram and Twitter.

REGIS ST LOUIS

Regis grew up in a small town in the American Midwest – the kind of place that fuels big dreams of travel – and he developed an early fascination with foreign dialects and world cultures. He spent his formative years learning Russian and a handful of Romance languages, which served him well on journeys across much of the globe. Regis has contributed to more than 50 Lonely Planet titles, covering destinations across six continents. His travels have taken him from the mountains of Kamchatka to remote island villages in Melanesia, and to many grand urban landscapes. When not on the road, he lives in New Orleans.

GREG WARD

Since whetting his appetite for travel by following the hippy trail to India, and later living in northern Spain, Greg Ward has written guides to destinations all over the world. As well as covering the USA from the Southwest to Hawaii, he has ranged on recent assignments from Corsica to the Cotswolds, and Japan to Corfu. See his website, www. gregward.info, for his favourite photos and memories.

Published by Lonely Planet Global Limited
CRN 554153
1st edition – Mar 2019
ISBN 978 1 7886 8274 9
© Lonely Planet 2019   Photographs © as indicated 2019
10 9 8 7 6 5 4 3 2 1
Printed in China